WITHDRAWN FROM
COLLECTION

LOST HOT RODS

Pat Ganahl

1961   1965   1970   1975

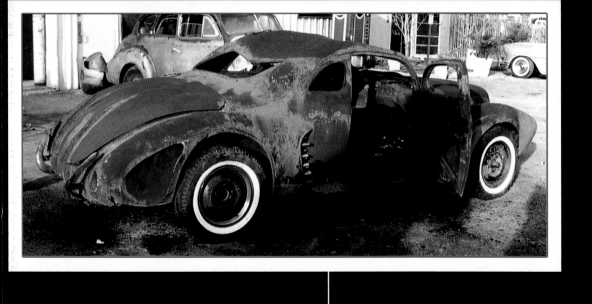

Remarkable Stories
of How They Were Found

***CarTech*®**
CarTech®, Inc.
39966 Grand Avenue
North Branch, MN 55056
Phone: 651-277-1200 or 800-551-4754
Fax: 651-277-1203
www.cartechbooks.com

Edit by Scott Parkhurst
Layout by Monica Seiberlich

ISBN 978-1-934709-22-1
Item No. CT487

Library of Congress Cataloging-in-Publication Data

Ganahl, Pat.
  Lost hot rods : remarkable stories of how they were found /
by Pat Ganahl.
    p. cm.
  Includes index.
  ISBN 978-1-934709-22-1
  1. Hot rods—History. I. Title.

  TL236.3.G3624 2010
  629.228'6—dc22

                                            2010009008

Printed in China
10 9 8 7 6 5 4 3 2 1

Front Cover:
*This '32 Ford Roadster was found tucked away in a Los
Angeles garage, pretty much untouched since being
modified in the late 1940s. While not a noteworthy car at
the time it was first built into a hot rod, it's state of
preservation makes it very desirable today. See page 122
for the whole story.*

Frontispiece:
Model A with a Chevy engine and Cragar wheels.

Title Page:
Bill Cushenberry's 1940 El Matador *Ford coupe.*

Back Cover Photos

Top Left and Top Right:
Joe Cruces Tall T.

Bottom Left and Bottom Right:
Tom Pollard's 1929 A Roadster.

OVERSEAS DISTRIBUTION BY:

Brooklands Books Ltd.
P.O. Box 146, Cobham, Surrey, KT11 1LG, England
Phone: 01932 865051 • Fax: 01932 868803
www.brooklands-books.com

Brooklands Books Aus.
3/37-39 Green Street, Banksmeadow, NSW 2109, Australia
Phone: 2 9695 7055 • Fax: 2 9695 7355

Contents

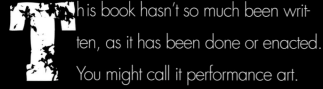**his** book hasn't so much been written, as it has been done or enacted. You might call it performance art.

Or, you might simply call it performance.

I called it "hot rod archeology" back in 1995, when I did an article called "The Grand Shop Tour," in issue No. 4 of *The Rodder's Journal*. I wrote about driving all over Los Angeles looking for the original sites of venerable speed shops and hot rod parts manufacturers, so I think I can lay claim to that term. This time—in this much-bigger story—I'm looking for old hot rods, all over the country. I could also call it "hot rod prospecting," but that has a connotation of striking it rich, monetarily, and that's not what this book is about at all. It's much more about the search, and hopefully the find; possibly about the resurrection, and maybe restoration. For me, it's more like catch-and-release fishing. It's also about a certain insatiable curiosity/hunger/itch that seems to be endemic to hot rodding—to all automotive enthusiasm, really—that I know well myself and see in and hear about from so many I've dealt with over many years.

Any true car person should relate to this. I don't know when it really began for me, but it was well before I could drive. I was a child of the 1950s, and during that decade cars were exciting, in themselves, and hopping them up or customizing them was part of the popular culture as strong as rock-and-roll music and burgers at the drive-in. I vividly remember when I saw my first hot rod. It was a white, channeled, flathead-powered roadster that was pulling into the local high school parking lot, and I was astounded to see how the cycle fenders on the front turned with the wheels as the driver steered into the driveway. This was a beach town, and another indelible image was a lowered, primered, full-fendered 1929 roadster pickup, filled with laughing teenage boys and girls, that came cruising through my neighborhood one day. It had a full-length "roof" (extending over the open cab), supported by bed stakes, that was loosely thatched with dried palm fronds! How could an impressionable 10-year-old forget something like that?

So about that time, I became an avid hot rod enthusiast, and part of the drill (especially being way too young to have a car of my own) was to learn every hot rod or custom in town, who owned it (by name), where it parked, and where it went when it inevitably got sold or bought (or wrecked, or parted out). On the way home from school my friends and I would check every garage door that was open a crack, peer over backyard fences (or through the slats). We always checked the back row of the used car dealers' lots and behind the few auto repair shops in town to see if anything new (or old) might show up. We got so good we could identify most of the local cars, from across town, whenever they'd fire up with headers or cutouts open: "Yeah, that's Charlie Lopez' 301 in his 1940 coupe. He's tuning the dual quads he just put on it. 'Gonna run it at Pomona this weekend."

Of course the same thing continued when I had a car to drive. Whether it was driving through my own town, passing through another one, or especially on longer trips to new territory, a hot rodder can't help peeking in any open garage, looking down alleys, and checking back lots. And, yes, I even looked behind barns, in sheds, and in every farm field that might possibly have a cluster of old cars/trucks/tractors/whatever out to pasture somewhere.

Not too long ago we called this stuff "vintage tin." Out in the West you'd look for it in the desert. In other parts of the country it'd be found in farm fields, barns, or in the woods. That's where both Grabowski and Ivo found the bodies for their famous Ts—sitting out in the desert, free for the taking. Well, that's not what this book is about. That kind of vintage tin doesn't exist anymore. The deserts and the farm fields have been picked clean of the good old stuff.

In the first place, this book is about vintage hot rods (and to a slightly lesser degree early customs and some drag cars), not the stock stuff. If you're looking for cars (or pickups) from the 1940s, 1950s, or 1960s, either in patina or still in nice original condition, to buy cheap and fix up into a cool rod or custom, there's plenty of that still around. But that's a different topic. In this book we're looking for well-known rods or customs, such as ones that were on magazine covers, which have simply disappeared and haven't been seen for decades. I also show you several cool cars built in the 1940s, 1950s, or 1960s that were never well known, but have been discovered recently either in excellent, fair, or at least rebuildable condition. Plus I show rods or customs that have been owned by the same person for 40 or 50 years, probably kept in the same garage, and have been little seen elsewhere. Also included are several that have been in the same owner/builder's garages that amount of time because, well, they've just never gotten finished. And there's still "lost treasure" out there to be found, such as the 1932 roadster or three-window that some grandfather or son or nephew left behind, that's been sitting in someone's driveway or garage—not out in the desert or a farm field—for 40 years. I have some examples to show.

I was also planning a chapter called "Recently Departed," about well-known rods of the 1970s, 1980s, or even 1990s that, say, won the Oakland Roadster Show, the Ridler Award at the Detroit Autorama, or were named Hot Rod of the Year or something similar and got on the covers of all the magazines, and then—poof—gone. Where did they go? There are dozens, if not hundreds, of such cars. My short list started with the Coddington-built Vern Luce 1933 Coupe, the similar Bob Reed 1934, Rick Dobbertin's ultimate Pro-Street Pontiac J2000 (made into a Revell model), Cole Cutler's flamed drag-racing 1934 street rod, Gary Kollofski's 1955 street Chevy, and the "Nickel Roadster" 1932 (*Rod & Custom* cover, April 1993).

I've spent an inordinate amount of time trying to track some of these down, with or without luck. As one example: For several years I saw the Vern Luce coupe sitting in the front window of the Assael BMW dealership in Monrovia, California, every time I passed on the 210 freeway. I consider this one of the most famous and influential hot rods ever, and had fully intended to include it in this book (especially since I knew where it was). Then one day I noticed the car was gone. Then the dealership changed names—this was a few years ago. Recently I located Dennis Assael (through the internet) to ask where the car was. He said he sold it some time ago "to the highest bidder" and didn't know where it went. Then, at this year's L.A. Roadster show, Thom Taylor (who designed the car) said some guy with an accent came up to him, asked if he was Thom, and said he had the coupe in Australia. Fortunately, Thom got his name and, after several tries, I was able to contact the owner in Melbourne. He said he'd had the car nearly ten years, and had driven it so much he was tearing it down for a rebuild. He promised to send me photos to include in this book, but that hasn't happened yet.

So you can see how it goes. New or old, tracking many of these "lost" cars down hasn't been easy.

My point is that this book has really been in the works for decades. Some of you who have memorized every car magazine you ever read might recognize a few of the cars shown here from small mentions I've made in magazine columns of the past.

Another thing I should point out here at the beginning is that the photography in this book isn't meant to be glamorous. We're all spoiled at this point by Steve Coonan's lush low-light photos. But when you're tracking lost cars, often hidden in dimly-lit garages piled with junk, and possibly in far-flung locations, you can't wait for sunset to take your pictures. In other cases I've had to rely on car owners in even more remote places to supply me with photos, which range from very good to edgy at best. The same goes for some of the "before" photos of these cars, from back in the day. But we who love searching for long-lost rods and customs have an affinity for old grainy photographs, don't we? I show you some of the older finds, and several that "got away," from during my years of doing this stuff. I hope you enjoy what follows. I did.

Where to Look

his quest that I sometimes call hot rod archeology can be fun and it can be rewarding, but it can also be frustrating. In this chapter, I give you some of my hard-learned knowledge about looking for lost hot rods.

Three Questions

In my many years of working at hot rod magazines, there are three questions I've heard constantly relating to this topic. First, obviously, is, "Whatever happened to such-and-such car?" This is the primary subject of this book, and I'll explore it from several angles. One of the things that really surprised me was how the topic grew. Naturally, I started with an extensive list of rods, customs, or race cars that I either knew existed, or I was simply curious to find. I was frustrated in several instances, to finally track a car down but not be able to actually see it or photograph it. On the other hand I was amazed and a bit overwhelmed at how the list multiplied. More often than not, when I located a famous (or not-famous) car in a garage, or shop, or wherever, the owner or the person who led me to it would say, "Well, if you're looking for this sort of thing, there's this car here, and that car there, and..." It's incredible how much of this stuff is still out there. More on this later.

The second question, quite naturally, is, "How can I find one of these early historical rods or customs myself?" Well, again, this book *shows* you how that's done, more than *tells* you, in a variety of ways. One of the first chapters is devoted to people I call "Finders," who have had a knack for locating—and in most cases, acquiring—highly desirable, or perhaps actually historic, vintage rods, customs, or race cars. I've asked each one of them to tell me their method, or their tricks, and every one simply says, "Nothing special," or, "I just find them." Read what they say and you'll learn a few things.

In England, a few years ago, they had a craze called *train-spotting*. What we're doing could be called

This 1932 Vicky is emblematic of one type of lost hot rod and helped instigate this book. I first saw it more than 25 years ago at a Burbank Road Kings car show, parked in the back, and I immediately recognized it from its feature in the October 1964 *Hot Rod*. The McCulloch-blown T-Bird engine and the grooved-wall Firestone slicks were give-aways. I couldn't find the owner then, or for the next two decades. When I finally tracked it down to include here, coincidentally so had *The Rodder's Journal*. You can read the full story in issue No. 45. But it still has the same black lacquer sprayed by Valley Custom's Clay Jensen, and the same air in those slicks that it had in 1964!

"car spotting," or even, "rod spotting." The similarities are that it requires a considerable amount of dedicated time and focus. This includes putting yourself in the places where the cars are likely to be found, both physically and/or communally. And, yes, there's a large element of luck, as you shall see, but it's usually not random or blind luck. As they say, it's more a case of being in the right place at the right time.

In slightly earlier days, there were several tricks that worked well. One of the best, back when the local newspaper's classified ads were effective, and the "Cars for Sale" section included the heading "Antiques and Classics," was to place a one-liner like: "Wanted, 1932 Ford, any condition," or, "Looking for old hot rod," or something to that effect. If you happen to live in a

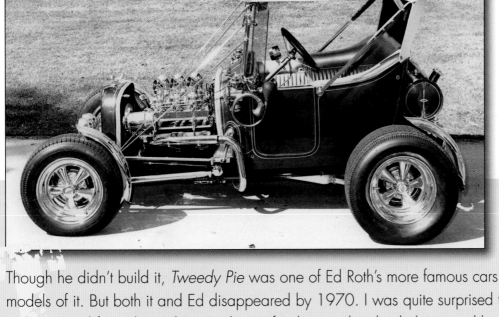

Though he didn't build it, *Tweedy Pie* was one of Ed Roth's more famous cars. They're still selling models of it. But both it and Ed disappeared by 1970. I was quite surprised to see the car reappear in the second form shown here (with top, fenders, wide wheels/tires, and lots more chrome, but still the same engine, paint, and Roth striping) at a meet sponsored by *Street Rodder* magazine (where I was then editor) called the Un-Nationals, held at Knott's Berry Farm in late 1975. The car was owned by Jack Lavoy and his 18-year-old son, Chris, who'd had it 13 years by then. Amazingly, I didn't know at that time that the "lost" Roth was working right there at Knott's, which is where I "found" him a year later (as reported in the June 1976 *Street Rodder*). In my book on Ed Roth (published in 2003 by CarTech), I said I had remained in contact with Chris, but the car was back in the same family garage where "it's been…close to 40 years, and it's definitely not for sale." Well, car collector Larry Tarantolo from Illinois had also been in contact with Lavoy and finally offered him enough money to change his mind. So I was very surprised to see it unexpectedly reappear, completely restored and repainted (by Roth acolyte/striper Shane Syx of Ohio), at a big Roth tribute display at the Detroit Autorama in 2006. Since then, however, Tarantolo resold the car at auction—"to finance new projects," he said—and it's now hidden away, again, in a private collection.

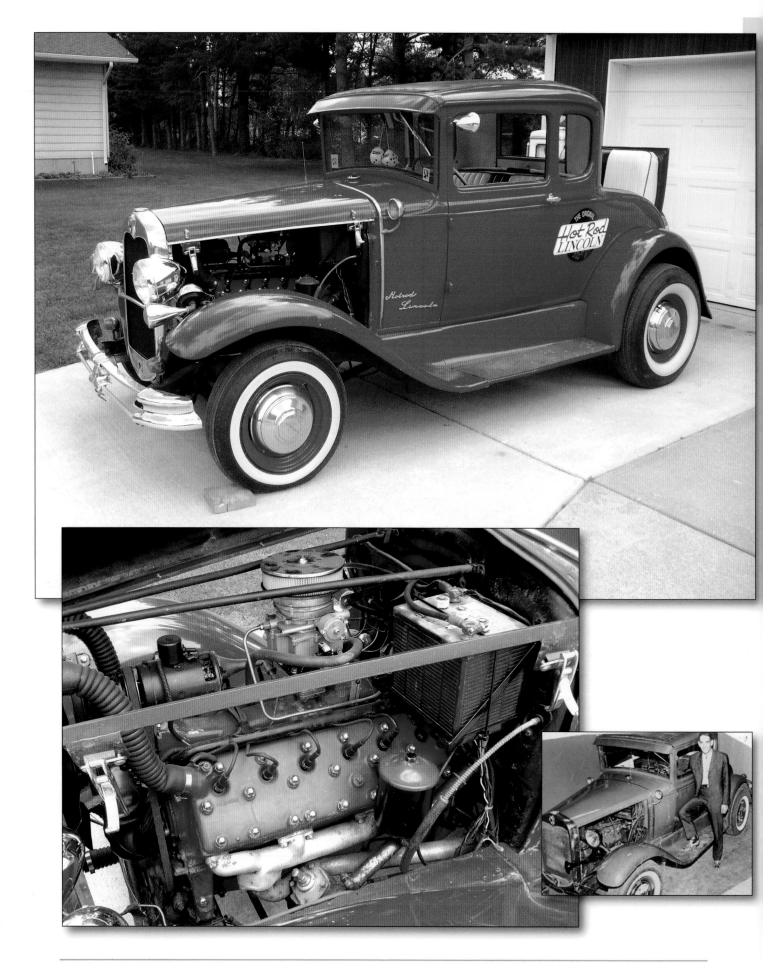

"Hot Rod Lincoln," with its twangy electric guitar and infectious beat—let alone the fact it was about a hot rod—was the first 45-rpm record I bought as a kid. Little did I know that its original writer and performer, Charlie Ryan, actually had such a car, with a Model A body and a Lincoln V-12 engine. The small, grainy photo shows Charlie on tour with it in 1960 and, yes, he built it himself. I think I learned about this when Bob Davidson, a customizer and body shop owner in Charlie's hometown of Tacoma, Washington, had volunteered his and several others' time and resources to help Charlie fully restore the car in 1980. At that time I met Charlie and his wife, Ruth, got the full story on the car, and did a three-page feature on it in the June 1990 issue of *Rod & Custom*. While researching this book (knowing Charlie had recently passed away), I traced the car to a small museum in northeast Washington, only to find that someone had just bought it—Larry Tarantolo. The current photos show this little-known, yet historic, hot rod as it arrived at Larry's recently. He and Dave Shuten plan a more period-correct re-restoration. And Larry swears this one is a keeper.

I have always loved the search for lost hot rods, not to acquire them (because I couldn't afford to), but partly for the fun of discovering them and partly just wishful thinking. In most cases I did my hunting with a camera. I call them "ones that got away." This first example is in just one corner of a large backyard stuffed with mostly early Ford, rod-related cars and parts. Behind the three-window is a pretty complete 1936 cabriolet; out of the picture is a chopped 1932 Vicky. This guy collected stuff from the 1940s through the 1980s, buying and selling at what I thought were high prices. Then he died and it all just disappeared. I went by one day and the yard was empty.

One of the first hot rods that turned me on was Tommy Ivo's low, red, and fast T-bucket with that wild, Hilborn-injected, nailhead Buick engine. I'd followed it through the dark-blue Bill Rowland version with cowl lights, but hadn't seen the Barris version when Hy Rosen of Riverside, California, owned it and it was featured in the April 1965 *Hot Rod*. Nearly a decade later, when I was dealing with Hy's son Jack at the family's business (Reliable Auto Wrecking/Auto Accessories), he told me his father still had the T at his house, partly disassembled. I had to go see it. The heads were off, and I was chagrinned to see all the button-tuck upholstery, fur carpet, and square headlights, but it was red again, it was all there, and in very good condition. There it sat, moved to a storage unit after Hy's passing, for another decade or more. Fortunately it finally did get properly restored and has been on display in the NHRA Museum since.

small town, with a surviving local paper, this could still work. But various sites on the internet don't usually work well in a "wanted" capacity. Instead, you can spend hours and days combing the numerous internet sites that list hot rods for sale, or even more hours and days searching the ones that list anything for sale, hoping to find that extremely rare listing for "1932 Ford roadster," or, more likely, "Old hot rod for sale." If it's something good, you have to be one of the first (of zillions) to call. But more likely you'll make a zillion calls before you find something that's actually good. The moral is that surfing the internet is not the best way to find a lost hot rod. It can work, but it's very time, labor, and luck intensive.

Here's just one old trick that might work better: If you know a lineman who works for the phone company (who climbs telephone poles and sees into lots of backyards every day), or a meter reader for the electric company, or even a mail carrier—anyone who goes house-to-house in neighborhoods on a regular basis—ask him if he's seen anything that looks like an old rod or custom sitting in a backyard, behind a garage, in a driveway, whatever. Remember that "old car" is a relative term. It might help if you show him a couple photos of examples of what you're looking for. If you really have time for this, then follow up any lead, and you might be surprised (or rewarded) for your efforts. On the other hand, here's a further tip: If

the person thinks he has seen the type of thing you're looking for, buy him a cheap disposable camera for him to take some pictures of it the next time he's in that neighborhood.

I could go on and on with such tips and tricks but, by the end of this book you learn that the most effective way to discover lost, old, or neglected rods or customs is by networking. This starts with being an involved hot rodder yourself, usually over an extended period of time. Joining a club helps a lot. If you hang around with other rodders, especially old-timers, you're going to hear about all sorts of hot rods hidden in garages or languishing, unfinished, in shops or in backyards. This is not about going to car shows or rod runs as a spectator and looking at the cars with "for sale" signs in the windows.

In fact, one of the most effective ways to find old, hidden hot rods or customs is to drive your own hot rod around, often. It's like trolling with bait. Especially today, when rods and customs are significantly older, and visually different than the rest of traffic, and there are very few on the streets, they draw immediate attention. Drive your hot rod to the grocery store, to the gas station, to church on Sunday, wherever; invariably, people come up to you wanting to know what year it is, how much it cost, how fast it goes, and similar predictable questions. But every so often someone says, "Hey, my grandpa has one just like that," or, "I've got one of those at home." Yes, it might turn out to be an old Jeep or dune buggy, but it just might turn out to be some long-lost custom or a Deuce three-window. I show examples here, and I've heard of plenty more.

This gold-and-brown Model A with frenched Chevy pickup taillights and Florida license could be seen, like this, from Broadway Avenue in Anaheim, in the mid 1970s. It had a Chevy engine and Cragar wheels. But when I knocked on the door of the older house and a lady answered, I could smell dozens of cats and see stacks of newspapers and other junk, with pathways, inside. She said I could go in the yard and take more pictures. It was her son's car, who was in the service, or something. But I knew it would be there a long time. She seemed to be what we call a "hoarder" today.

This was another equally strange, but more tempting, case in a nearby neighborhood. This Deuce three-window with leaded-in 1950 Ford taillights sat in a driveway behind a Mustang and a Pinto, each with one front fender removed. The 1932 had a filled shell, full hood, and was cherry. I could never find anybody home. Then one evening I saw the guy drive up—he worked late hours in the Coroner's Department in L.A. Of course, nothing was for sale. He showed me a backyard full of early Ford parts. The cars sat in the driveway for a few years. Then he built a big tin shed in the backyard and moved everything into it.

I'd heard that a guy who owned a small trucking company had an old racing GMC six with a Howard 12-port head that he might sell. Yep, he showed me the four-carb mill, complete and stored in a packing shed, but he couldn't come up with a price. Then he said, "Want to see the car it was in?" and took me to a newer garage up front where I saw this nice 1930 Chevy coupe with a complete tri-carb J-2 Olds engine, wedged between a Corvette, a boat, and a snowmobile. That's a bean-bag chair on the roof. I drove by the place for years, figuring it was still in there. Now nobody in the area knows where it went.

The third question I hear a lot these days is, "What is my car's history?" This curiosity opens a whole new topic, with several offshoots, that is a relatively recent development in hot rodding but is also germane to this book in a couple of ways. First, let's try to approach it succinctly: Originally, hot rods and customs had no history. People were cutting up Henry's or GM's finest models and modifying them beyond recognition, to every restorer's horror. Further, and more pertinent to our topic, these early rods and customs needed to be constantly remodified and updated. Rodding, back then, was a trend-driven exercise in a trendy time. After you built a rod or custom in the prevailing style, if you kept it for any length of time, you'd have to keep updating it to remain cool at the local drive-in or annual car show. Steel wheels with hubcaps gave way to chrome wheels, which gave way to mags. White tuck-and-roll gave way to black, which gave way to (ugh!) button-tuft. As always, the newer trend was not necessarily better.

Car shows exacerbated this. If you won your class one year (or if you didn't), you had to do more to your car to get more points to do better, or beat competitors, the next time. Many show promoters actually required a specific number of changes to a car (sometimes including a new color) for it to be allowed in the next year's show, figuring spectators wouldn't pay to see the same cars again. Thus, especially during the 1960s, many hot rods became overchromed and undriven show cars, while others that were more into weekend performance became full-on, towed-to-the-track drag cars. And drag cars, as in any form of racing, had to updated, rebuilt, or replaced constantly to remain competitive.

This is one I really wish I hadn't let get away. In the late 1950s/early 1960s, Richard King owned a body shop behind a gas station in my hometown, and this car, which looked like a sectioned and shortened 1955 Chevy, often sat out front. We paid little attention to it at the time because King was an older guy and, with its Continental kit, two-tone paint, wide whites and wheelcovers, it wasn't a cool custom of the time. It wasn't until years later that I found it was featured in one of the "little mags" and learned that it was all hand-built on a 1954 Corvette chassis, complete with the rare three-carb 'Vette six. Here's the kicker: Sometime in the 1980s or 1990s, I was driving out on the 60 freeway near the small town of Glen Avon and saw this car, exactly like this, sitting on a hill with a "for sale" sign on it. I didn't stop. When I went back, it was gone. Nobody knew anything about it. I even went back recently, with a photo of it, asking anybody in the area having anything to do with cars if they had seen it. Nope. Where did it go? Lost.

Here's a totally different story that some of you might know. The Joe Nitti 1932 roadster, titled *Deep Purple*, was featured on one black-and-white page in a 1950 *Hot Rod* magazine, but many rodders, including me, have since venerated it. When I got my own 1932, I wanted to make mine similar, including deep-purple paint. But none of us had ever seen color pictures of the car, so I decided to try to find it. After tons of research and contacts with many people who knew Joe and the car at the time, I couldn't trace it beyond 1952. I told as much as I could find out in a 10-page article in *The Rodder's Journal* No. 9. Besides curiosity and the fun of the hunt, I mainly wanted to find out what color purple it was. But someone else thought I was trying to buy it. He had more time and better detective skills than I, and he actually found, and bought, the car in Sacramento, and had it fully restored. I asked him to send me a chip of the original purple, but he didn't. He since resold the car to Mark Mountanos of Ukiah, California, who had to repaint the car again before showing it at the 75th Deuce Anniversary display. The car is now in Mountanos' private collection, and I'm showing a black-and-white photo of it because I still don't know exactly what the original color was.

Historic Hot Rods?

The point is two-fold. First, the thought of preserving one of these early rods, customs, or race cars—let alone ever *restoring* one—was simply out of the question back then. No one dreamed this would ever happen.

Consequently, second, it is utterly amazing that so many of these early cars still exist, in anything close to their so-called original or historic forms. Think about it. Besides the reasons given above for the constant changing and updating of these cars, consider that rods and customs are *personalized* vehicles. Any time one got sold to a new owner, which was frequently, that person wanted to make it his or her own, to make new creative changes to it. That's the nature of customizing.

In the case of drag or lakes cars, it's more pragmatic: There's nothing worth less than an outmoded race car. If it's no longer competitive or doesn't meet the new season's rules, what are you going to do with it? No one wants to buy it and, especially in the case of lengthy dragsters, they aren't easy to store. So most had any viable parts stripped and reused, with the frame cut up and thrown away. Or did they? Given the incredible number of 1950s and 1960s dragsters that are being found and restored today (including just a few representative examples in this book), maybe the fact that they were unmarketable helped save them—that and a bit of sentimentality, combined with shops or garages big enough to hang them from the walls or rafters. It's truly amazing that so many still exist.

Here are a couple more things to consider. The first is storage. You're not going to save an old rod or custom unless you have someplace to keep it. That's why it was logical to look in barns to start with. Barns are big and easy to store stuff in—like an old car that wore out, and wasn't worth trading in, but you really liked, and you might want to fix up some day or give to your son or grandson. The chances of that car being a Corvette or Ferrari, or a rod or custom, are slim. However, a lot more people live in cities or suburbs than live on farms. Consequently, more people who own rods or customs live in these places. And most of these people live in houses with garages. Whether they (or you) want to admit it, a large percentage of the garages in America are used for storage rather than a place to park the daily-driver automobile, right? It's been this way for decades. Plus, barns are dusty, often leaky, and known to house rodents that gnaw on things. A garage is a much cleaner, safer place to store something you want to save or keep in decent condition.

You've undoubtedly read about the incredible find of Ed Roth's *Orbitron* in Mexico recently, and I show a couple more Roth finds later. But the one that I would love to own, and has eluded discovery, is this 1930 Model A from his early days, called *Little Jewel*. It was red when Roth owned it, with Olds power, but I like it best in this lime green with white pearl scallops by Ed after he sold it to Henry Cantu. The last time I saw it was in the spectator lot at the 1962 Winternationals; the hood was off and a small-block Chevy had just been installed. It hasn't been seen anywhere since, but I have a hunch it's in Henry Cantu's garage.

And that brings us to the second consideration: sentimentality. If you've built a hot rod or custom car yourself, or even bought one already built and then personalized it further, you aren't going to trade it in, sell it, or otherwise get rid of it like any old car. In the old days, rods or customized cars had zilch trade-in value, and selling one inevitably got you a fraction of the cost to build it. Worse, an out-of-style rod or custom was worth about as much as an uncompetitive race car. When it wasn't going to win any more trophies, either at the car show or the strip, you probably parked it in the garage, figuring you'd rebuild it someday or maybe your son would. That's why urban or suburban garages are the most likely places to find lost hot rods, rather than barns, deserts, or farm fields. One further point I hesitate to mention is that hot rodding is only two or three generations old today. That means that many of these long-stored hot rods are now being inherited by wives, sons, grandsons, or other relatives who probably don't have the same sentimental attachment to them as the original owner/builder, and might not even understand or appreciate what they are.

Provenance and Value

I do not want to suggest in this book that tracking down lost hot rods is some sort of treasure hunt that leads to quick riches. As I say, the idea of hot rods being historic, or collectible, or having any sort of "provenance" was unthinkable 20 or so years ago. But the fact is that hot rods have finally been invited to Pebble Beach, vintage dragsters have won AACA top class awards, and more and more of these cars are being collected and restored in very exacting detail for large sums of money.

I have stated elsewhere my dislike for Pebble Beach hot rods and for concours collectors buying up historic rods, customs, or dragsters at high prices. So I won't dwell on it here. But I have to admit it's a double-edged sword. Many truly famous or noteworthy rods and similar vehicles have been unearthed, saved and/or restored, and are now in some sort of public museums where they can be appreciated by future generations. This is good. In fact, since Jim Jacobs found and restored the Niekamp roadster (the first Oakland AMBR winner) some 40 years ago, drove it all over the country, showed it at Pebble Beach the first time hot rods were invited, and finally sold it to the Petersen Automotive Museum where people can see it today, hundreds of other such cars have been famously found, restored, and preserved.

I assume you know about these well-publicized vehicles, such as the majority of the Ed Roth vehicles, most of the famous Barris custom Mercurys, a large percentage of the past Oakland AMBR winners, and even most of the 75 Most Significant 1932 Ford Hot Rods that were feted by Ford Motor Company at the Pomona Grand National Roadster Show on their 75th

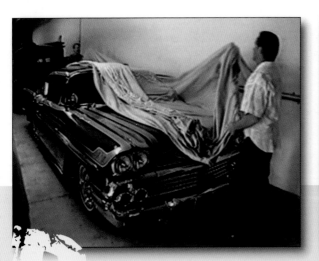

Please excuse the graininess of these photos, but I had to take them from a DVD version of my video. This is Mox Miller's amazing panel-painted and fully chromed 1958 Impala, which I discuss later. Besides uncovering it and the matching 1958 pickup then, the only other time he's had it out was for a photo feature for Steve Coonan in *The Rodder's Journal* No. 32. The Impala hasn't run since about 1962, and it is still perfect. But it stays covered up in a huge garage behind Mox's house. Lost.

anniversary in 2007. In the field of drag racing, cars like the Greer-Black-Prudhomme dragster, the Tony Nancy 1929 roadsters, and literally hundreds more from front-engine rails to Funny Cars have been found, featured in magazines, and put on display in the Don Garlits or NHRA Wally Parks museums. They were brought out to again "cackle" on nitro at the highly popular Hot Rod Reunion meets. I have one of these in my own garage, in fact. These cars are no longer lost, even if they once were. They've been featured in other books. I assume you know about them.

This book is about the huge number of slightly less famous, to completely unknown, hot rods and their kin still lurking in garages or lingering in shops that you *don't* know about. One caveat I must mention here, however, is that the process of researching, writing, and then producing this book—requiring a significant amount of travelling around the country finding and photographing many of these cars—took much more than a year. During this time some of the cars that were lost when I found them have been subsequently discovered by magazine editors and rushed into print, or have even been brought out, cleaned up, and put back on the car-show or rod-run scene by owners (or new owners) who are excited to have

attention paid to these cars again. I have eliminated a couple of such cars from the book. If others don't seem so "lost" by the time you read this, understand that they were when I found them.

One way to entice a long-lost rod or custom out of hiding, especially one with some so-called provenance retained by the same owner for decades, is to offer a huge amount of money for it. I figure that option is out of the question for the vast majority of people. Worse, in my personal opinion, are the wily hunters and stalkers who have the time to track down such cars, and have enough money to induce the long-time owners (or their widows, etc.) to finally let go of them. These operators know that they can either quickly restore them or sell them, as-is, for some large multiple of their buying price, either at today's amazing car auctions or directly to known, well-heeled, private collectors. Such buyers are known in the real estate business as "flippers." It's part of the capitalist agenda, which is one of our American freedoms, so I say no more about that here.

However, many of our once-famous or well-known rods, customs, or race cars have, for the various reasons stated above, disappeared once again into private high-dollar car collections or mini-museums that are

The Hirohata Merc has been seen so much since being meticulously restored by owner Jim McNiel that I almost forgot how lost it was and how desperately people were seeking it. I was finally able to announce its discovery in *Rod & Custom* in August 1989. In this case I knew a couple people who knew where it was, but were sworn to secrecy, and I had to badger them until they'd tell. Then I had to convince Jim that we (the magazine) wanted to help *him* restore the car. This photo was taken in his garage, after he had rebuilt the engine and chassis, but before he started stripping the paint.

I was going to include a whole chapter called "Recently Departed," showing many rods and customs that gained fame in the last couple of decades and then—poof—disappeared. The Thom Taylor–designed, Boyd Coddington–built, Vern Luce coupe is arguably the most famous and influential rod of the past quarter-century, or more. I named it one of the Top-20 All-Time Rods and Customs in the August 1990 issue of *Rod & Custom* and didn't get any arguments. I'm showing a black-and-white photo of it here because it's on the street, Boyd is driving, and everybody knows it's red. We recently discovered it's now owned by Gary Brown of Melbourne, Australia, who has driven it so much he has it torn down for a rebuild. The similar, red, Chrome Shop coupe owned by Bob Reed of Poteau, Oklahoma, won the Detroit Autorama Ridler Award in 1984, but has been seen little since. Greg Fleury, who built it, has no idea where it is. Jim "Bones" Noteboom, who owned it briefly in the early 1990s, says he thinks some collector in the Ventura, California, area has it.

accessible only to the owners and their personal friends. Such collections have always existed, all around the world, but they were usually comprised of rare, expensive, high-end collector cars. It is only recently that I've noticed the development of a generation of such collectors, who remember having or being fascinated by hot rods in their youth, and who have the wherewithal to collect them today. You've probably seen two or three books recently about amazing garages full of such personal car collections, but these don't begin to give you any idea of the number and scope of such private collections today. I've known about many for years, but I was astounded by how many more I discovered as I was researching this book. They're everywhere. They have incredible cars in them, now including hot rods or customs in many cases, and ranging from 50 to 200 vehicles in a single collection.

The good news is that such "lost" rods and customs are being preserved. The bad news is that, at present, the general public can't see or appreciate them. And you can't afford to buy them because their prices appreciate unrealistically each time they are sold. So, for the most part, such lost rods won't be included in this book, and I truly hope that cars uncovered in this book don't end up being re-lost into such private collections. To some extent it is inevitable, but it's not what this book is about. I do, however, highly commend the few collectors who regularly drive their collector rods to events, show them in public museums, and/or regularly invite other rodders to see their collections. You may know who they are (and they certainly do).

Instead, this book is about the fun—the thrill—of finding a neat, old, lost rod or custom, just the way it is for an archeologist to uncover significant, historical, and lost artifacts. Your finding it might induce the owner to get it out, fix it up, and drive it again. If it happens to be for sale at a price you can afford, so much the better. Depending on its condition and its history, you might want to preserve it as-is (though hopefully in drivable form), clean and fix it up, or completely restore it. You could possibly restore it to a former version when it appeared in magazines, won shows, or smoked its tires down a dragstrip.

My "To Find" List

I've told you about my fascination with finding hot rods since I was a kid, and how networking is one of the best ways to find them. Well, what better position could someone be in to indulge in this pursuit than an editor of a hot rod magazine? Luckily I've been blessed to be such most of my working life, so I've been doing this for quite a while, this thing I call "hot rod archeology." The first person I worked for in this business was Tom McMullen, and when I found

out he was the guy who had that flamed, blown 1932 roadster from the cover of *Hot Rod*, my first question to him was, "Where is it now?" He was into choppers at that time but he told me where it might be. So I went and found it, in pieces (as shown in *Street Rodder*, June 1975). It took three decades before this car finally got restored to its famous condition. For me, the fun was finding it, photographing it, and showing readers where it was.

Another thrilling find for me was the Tommy Ivo T-bucket. I can't remember who told me where it was, but I photographed it in Hy Rosen's garage in Riverside, California, where it had been sitting for 10 years, and showed it in the November 1977 *Street Rodder*. In that same editorial I showed the last photo of Grabowski's T before it went to Jim Street's in Ohio (where it still sits), and I openly asked why these and other famous "lost" hot rods weren't being found and restored or put back on the street. I visited the Ivo T many times when it sat in storage at Rosen's, but somehow got scooped by another magazine when it finally got restored decades later. The point is: It finally got restored.

The same thing with *Ala Kart*. I think it was Gene Winfield who told me it was in Phoenix and gave me some clues. After much sleuthing and calling, I finally located the owner, who had it stored in aged but original condition, and told him I would come to Phoenix just to get a photo of it. No dice. He wouldn't even open the storage shed door. Same thing with Roth's *Tweedy Pie*. I kept in contact with owner Chris Lavoy for many years, even going to his garage where it was kept, but he wouldn't let me see it. Both cars were finally pried loose from their long-time keepers by large sums of money. One has been beautifully, and publicly, restored. The other got flipped after a couple brief public showings, and is now in a private collection.

In the May 1978 issue of *Street Rodder,* I showed a picture of the George Cerny chopped 1949 Plymouth wagon, along with two other early customs, as they sat in a storage yard in Redlands, California. That editorial, again, was about finding and saving such lost rods or customs, saying, "The point is...that a ton of these types of cars are still around and are usually available." Back then, that was definitely true. But not many took my advice, at that time.

As I would hear about such cars, especially if I got a name and a phone number or address, I'd write it on a slip of paper and put it next to my phone. I'd also do this if I got curious about where a certain car was, and wanted to track it down. As I got more clues, I'd add to my "Cars to Find" note stack next to the phone. I've done this at various magazine offices, and I still do it at home today. In many cases I found the cars and showed them in "Roddin' At Random" or similar columns. Others sat in the "To Find" pile for years.

One example was Mox Miller's fabulous panel-painted 1958 Impala. I'd remembered seeing it, with his dad's matching 1958 Chevy pickup, at one of the last L.A. car shows. I couldn't remember Mox's name, so I called my pal Greg Sharp, who was still on the L.A.P.D. force at that time and (in those pre-9/11 days) could access files of names, license plates, etc. He located a Moxom Miller, gave me an address and phone number, and I put it in the stack. It wasn't until I was making my first (and only) hot rod video in 1994 that I finally got a chance to call the number, connect with Mox, and go see and, literally, uncover this amazingly preserved car, all of which was captured on tape. Since it was shown there, as well as later profiled in *The Rodder's Journal*, it is only briefly shown here. But now it's covered up again.

Kirk Brewer's 1932

Here's a great example, in a time capsule, of hot rod archeology. Kirk Brewer was the John Milner of my hometown (Corona, California). He had the hottest car, he built it himself, and it was a 1932 Ford five-window coupe with a Corvette small-block with dual quads, tube headers, and a 4-speed. He actually got the car (for $150!) in 1960, before he could drive, but had it ready to run in the configuration described (black primer with chrome wheels) in that magic year of 1962. It ran low 13s at 110 at the track and it was his daily high-school driver. Everybody in town knew "Brewer's Deuce." By his senior year (1963), he painted it Chevy's brilliant Anniversary Gold and chromed the whole front suspension. But, because it was the new trend, within months he jacked up the front with a chromed-and-drilled Model A axle, added new American mags, and repainted it a metallic aqua. That's where I lost track of the car and Kirk because, unlike Milner, he did go to college (up in San Jose, California), and took the Deuce with him.

So, I'm not sure why, but when I started working for *Street Rodder* magazine, one of the first things I decided to do was find Kirk and find out whatever happened to his 1932. This was nearly a decade later. It turned out he was living and working in the San Francisco Bay area. I went up there, and he had a scrapbook showing how the car looked when he first got it, in black primer after he installed an Olds V-8 with the early Ford driveline and a dropped axle. It had chromies on the back, wide whites on the front, and 1958 Chevy Biscayne taillights. He also had snapshots showing the car in a dark-blue metallic, and then a striking dark-blue Metalflake, with a more tractable 4-barrel 327 in front of a chromed firewall. In this form it took first in class at the San Jose car show.

But by then Kirk was graduating from college, had married, and decided to sell the Deuce to the young nephew of someone he knew back home. The new owner had it painted cinnamon with dark flames, drove it to high school, and then parked it in his mom's garage when he got drafted. That's all Kirk knew. But he did have a handwritten bill of sale, dated 1960, with the name and address of the person he bought it from: Salvador Rivera.

This was 1974, but after a few phone calls I was able to find him and trace the car back through two or three prior owners to Johnny Moramarko of Fontana, California, who told me how he got it from a farmer's yard in sad shape, then filled the top, filled and peaked the grille, molded in a 1936 dash, added 1941 Ford bumpers and chromed Kelsey wires, and painted it red. By 1951, it had dropped sealed beams and bent front fenders. I included all this in a three-page article in the September 1974 issue of *Street Rodder* magazine titled, "Biography of a Street Rod."

I can't remember how I found the car's then-current location, though I wrote, "a friend mentioned...that it was stored in a garage..." That may have been a car, club buddy. But I did find it at the home of Merwin Lewis in Costa Mesa, California, who had recently bought it off the famous Stick City lot on Whittier Boulevard. The only thing he added were the black button-tufted running boards to match the interior. That was 35 years ago.

Of course I tried relocating the car today—not so easy. It had black-and-yellow plates, which would still be current in California if kept registered, but no

luck there. I even knew a couple of private investigators who looked into it, but nothing. I searched many sites on the Internet, as well as 1932 Ford registries, but found nothing. In all my years of attending rod events, I hadn't seen it. So I tried modern networking. This 1932 has (or had) several unique features: the filled roof, the chrome drip rails, the 1958 Chev taillights, the flat chromed firewall, and most significantly the molded 1936 dash filled with 1958 Corvette gauges. I posted this description on the H.A.M.B. forum of the *Jalopy Journal* website, along with photos of the car, where tens, if not hundreds, of thousands of hot rod viewers would see them. Nada. Nothing.

This is a prime example of how this hot rod archeology can be rewarding or frustrating. If you know where this is today, contact the publiher. I'd love to know.

Cars in My

I'm sure you've gathered by reading this far that a strong theme of this book is that lost famous hot rods, or just old neglected ones, are much more likely to be found in suburban garages, urban warehouses, or shops than in farmers' barns or fields. In the first place, as I've said, it's a matter of numbers. A whole lot more people live in cities and suburbs than live on farms. Most of them have garages, and store things in them that they want to save, for whatever reasons.

Second, the search is for neglected or hidden-away hot rods, customs, or related race cars, not just old vehicles in general. I may not have stressed this strongly enough yet. In our consumerist, throw-away society, automobiles are at the top of the list. We are programmed, in fact pressured, to get rid of an older car as soon as it gets a bit shabby, and buy a new more-modern one. There's virtually no incentive to save the old one. In fact, today there are strong incentives to crush it, melt it down, and recycle it. You love your new car, not the one it's replacing. And if you live in a neighborhood, you've usually got to get rid of the old car, hopefully to help pay for the new one, but also because there's only so much space to park vehicles. Many cities, my own included, have laws that you can't park an undriven vehicle for more than, say, three days in the street in front of your own house. And many cities have laws against parking unused vehicles anywhere in your yard.

If you live in the country or a rural area, however, you have room to store vehicles and you probably need a truck, a tractor, or a trailer or two. Vehicles in such areas tend to get used harder and longer than

Neighborhood

My neighbor Frank lives on the main road of our canyon and his garage is in the backyard. Unless both the gate and garage door are open, you'd never know there is a pair of nice sedans in there. Of all the cars in the neighborhood, these are really the least "lost." Frank travels a lot for work and spotted the humpback 1937 sedan, covered, in a yard in Iowa. It was cherry; it had belonged to the family since new; and, yes, it was for sale. He shipped it to a friend near Chicago and had him rebuild it with a Mustang II suspension, a 350/350, 9-inch rear, and the dove-gray paint. It rides on red wire wheels with a unique hood ornament found in a Midwest antique store. He found the black 1940 Standard as-is in Texas. It's obviously pro-built with similar driveline and suspension (painted red) and a bright red interior. I see Frank and family cruising the 1937 fairly often, and he takes the black '40 out late at night for stress-relief runs. Good medicine!

urban commuter cars. So when it's time to buy a new one, the old one has very little monetary value. And, A) you might need it for something some day; B) more likely you have one or more children growing toward driving age who might want it or at least could learn to drive in it; or C) given its lack of value, it's just easier to park it behind the barn or under a tree than it is to get rid of it.

If such vehicles sit long enough, they can actually begin to attain value, or even become collectible. So there's a large segment of auto enthusiasts who love hunting for these old cars or trucks, either to score one for themselves or to buy and sell them for profit. Hot rodders, as I've said, have always done this too, looking for what used to be called "vintage tin," or rod or custom "potential." Well, the vintage tin you can find in such rural settings isn't nearly as vintage as it once was. And, guess what? You're likely to find more old Model Ts, As, Fortys, or even a Deuce or two in neighborhood garages these days than you are in farm fields. In these cases, such vintage tin is usually known as an "older restoration."

Or they might be what are called "special interest autos"—Corvettes, T-Birds, Jaguars, Ferraris, Cobras, Panteras, or even Camaros or Mustangs—that have been squirreled away in such garages so long that their scarcity and value has increased, sometimes tremendously. There are as many of these in my neighborhood as there are hot rods. But this is not what this book is about.

My point is that, for the most part, the vehicles that are parked in barns, farm fields, or other rural areas are usually so-called stockers, and of little value when put there. If you're looking for an older, inexpensive car or pickup to fix up or modify, rural areas are a good place to look. But special vehicles, like a rod or custom, a restored Model T or A, a near-virgin 1932 or 1934, or even a Porsche or Corvette, are more likely to be found stored in suburban garages or other urban areas. They are either indoors or under wraps, where people tend to store things they want to keep.

Third, hunting for lost hot rods is a lot more fun. There's a yellow 1965 Stingray Corvette in a garage a few blocks away, up the hill. I think it's a big-block; it has the factory side pipes and aluminum wheels. I used to see it regularly (sitting, not driving), but for the last five years or so the garage door has been closed. If I were a Corvette lover, this would be a find. But I'm a hot rodder, and if I had it, I'd want to modify it, which would actually decrease its value these days. I don't need to press the argument that rodding and customizing are more fun than pure restoration, because you can do what you want, creatively. No, the point I want to make is that the yellow Corvette, though a fun vehicle and increasing in value as it sits, is still just one of thousands. Somebody bought it new, enjoyed driving it for awhile, and then parked it for some reason.

This is more like what you can find in garages all across America. Neighbor Randy moved in about 15 years ago and kept a pair of nice, 4-speed 1956 Chevys under car covers in the street, driving the dark-blue-and-white one to Bob's Drive-In every Friday night and to local shows. One day I saw his garage door open and I thought I spied a partially built Nomad inside. When I stopped by recently, he said he found a place to store the 1956s, but opened the garage to show me this black 1957 Bel Air two-door post. He said he got it like this, with fresh paint, built 350 and 4-speed, power disc brakes, power steering, and new stock upholstery. He has all the parts, but hasn't done anything further since he put it there. Now get this: As we were talking, another neighbor, seeing the door open, stopped to see what was going on. He said he lived around the corner and had a 1957 convertible in his garage, with the 270-hp dual-quad engine, that was almost done. That's one I've never even seen.

A vintage hot rod or custom car, on the other hand, had to have been built by someone. By definition, it is a unique vehicle. It's the only one exactly like it. Consequently, it has a personal story that goes with it. Who built it? When? Why did the owner build it this way? How many people have owned it, and what changes did they make? Even if this car never made it into a magazine, trophied in a car show, or won a drag race, it still has a history all its own. If this car did happen to be featured on the cover of a magazine, win a major car show, or gain fame in some other way in the past, and you or I have been able to track it down (or stumble across it), that means its history is that much more significant and finding it is that much more meaningful and fun. That's what this book is about.

I have chosen many of the "found" rods and customs featured here because of their fascinating and sometimes amazing stories, if not for their one-time fame.

Here's the killer: About 10 years ago my neighbor Paul asked me to go look at a 1940 Ford coupe a friend of his kept in a garage up the hill, to give him an idea of what it was worth. He said his mother bought it new, in town, and he had just had the engine rebuilt, some rewiring, a new headliner, and new tires put on it. I went to see it and was astounded. You could tell the trunk and one front fender had been bumped and repaired at some point, but the original black paint was shiny—even on the floorboards underneath! The seat was stained, but all the rest of the interior was original. The rebuilt engine had a tapping lifter, but still—talk about cherry. I hesitated to estimate its value, because I figured this was one hidden secret I'd keep to myself. It had new dual exhausts, so all it needed was a dropped axle and a couple of carbs. Turns out he drove it to our annual downtown car show once, but it overheated coming back up the hill, so he parked it and it hasn't moved since, as you see. When I went up to take these pictures recently, the owner was happy to show it to me, but announced as I was leaving, "This car is worth $200,000 in Japan. I'm going to sell it there and retire on the money." Okay. Looks like it's going to stay in the family at least one more generation.

The ones shown in this chapter, however, while they each have their own story, are presented as simple proof that the best place to start looking for lost hot rods is right in your own neighborhood. None of these cars are famous, but the sheer number I found is quite impressive. It's not unique to my neighborhood. I could do it most anywhere. In fact, everywhere I went finding and photographing cars for this book, the owner (or a neighbor or a friend who dropped by) would say, "Well, if you're looking for cars like this, there's this one here...and that one there, and..." Believe me; I left out more than I could fit in this one book.

The message here is that people don't throw away, trade-in, or crush old rods or customs; they store them in their garages, or similar safe, relatively clean places. Plus, this book is more about showing than telling, so let's get to it.

First, I'll briefly describe the locale. This neighborhood could be in the flat San Fernando Valley, or in the floodplain of Orange County, but it happens to be in a canyon on the east side of Glendale, California. This isn't one of the famous canyons of L.A. that once sheltered 1960s rock stars. It's not an art colony. And it isn't a hippie haven. It's a pretty typical, middle-class suburban southern California neighborhood that happens to be ringed by brush-covered ridges on three sides. One main road runs about 2 miles up the canyon, with a secondary one (mine) parallel to it, which dead-ends at the top and stops at a small school at the bottom. Most of the houses in the canyon (along these two streets) were built in the 1920s through the early 1940s, and range from large, two-story, now-expensive ones to very small ones with one-car garages. Ours, like most, is in-between. There are maybe a dozen smaller streets that branch off the main two, with houses built in the 1950s and 1960s a little higher up the hillsides.

Though there are deer, skunks, raccoons, and coyotes in the surrounding hills, our house is only five minutes from downtown Glendale, and 7 miles, as the sea gull flies, from Los Angeles City Hall. There are many people who have lived in this canyon all their lives, and many others who have moved in more recently from all parts of the world. I moved here in

As I was coming back from photographing the Forty, a block away I saw a garage door open with this inside. I had seen jacked-up 4x4 pickups parked there, with dune buggies and ATCs on trailers (plus the car under the cover is a Maserati), but this 1936 Chevy coupe was a surprise. I stopped to inquire, and the lady of the house said it was her husband and son's new project. They had gone to a rod meet somewhere a few years ago, decided these cars were cool, and found this one on eBay. As you can see, they have the tools to work on it, but she wasn't sure how much they had done. It has most of the usual aftermarket street rod components in place. But that was about a year ago, and I haven't seen the door open since.

1983, and I should mention that our house (built in 1937) had a two-car garage, which I've enlarged to hold five cars, in the large backyard. Most people in the neighborhood know me as "the guy with the old cars." Two or three drop by to see what's going on in the garage. But I want to stress that, unlike other parts of Glendale, or nearby Burbank or Eagle Rock, our neighborhood has never been a hotbed of hot rod activity, by any means. It's just a typical, middle-class suburban neighborhood that could be most anywhere in the United States.

The surprising part is how many cars are hidden in garages here. It's surprising, but it isn't unusual. I'm pretty sure that if you look in your own neighborhood, or similar ones, you'll find the same thing. Obviously, living in a neighborhood for some time, getting to know neighbors, driving up and down side streets, and (in my case) driving a hot rod or so-called old car of

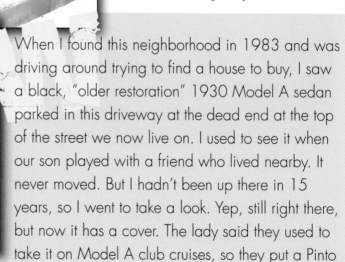

your own leads to finding (or finding out about) others. I've known about several of these cars for a long time. But others I just happened to see (or was told about) just recently.

Here's one tip: Since most of these cars are stored in garages, you won't see them unless the garage door happens to be open. So the best time to cruise such neighborhoods looking for hot rod treasure is on the weekends, or even in the evenings when people are coming home from work. And if the garage door is open, look very carefully. A treasured old car might be hiding under a typical car cover, but just as likely it might be draped with sheets, blankets, or even piles of boxes, suitcases, or lawn chairs. Look carefully. You could very well be surprised at what's in there.

Another thing I did in my neighborhood was to look for houses (especially older ones) where the daily cars are parked in the driveway or out front, and the garage doors have obviously been shut for a long time. In such cases you have to be bold, knock on the front door, and ask politely if there might be an old car in there. Again, you might be surprised.

Finally, not all of the hot rods I found in my neighborhood are really "lost" (they're just seldom seen driving on the street), while others are more "potential" than hot rods. But what I think is impressive is that I could find this many cars of definite hot rod interest, in the course of a few weeks, and all within a few blocks of my house (about 1/4-mile radius). And here's the kicker: Besides the Corvette I mentioned, there's plenty more stuff in my

When I found this neighborhood in 1983 and was driving around trying to find a house to buy, I saw a black, "older restoration" 1930 Model A sedan parked in this driveway at the dead end at the top of the street we now live on. I used to see it when our son played with a friend who lived nearby. It never moved. But I hadn't been up there in 15 years, so I went to take a look. Yep, still right there, but now it has a cover. The lady said they used to take it on Model A club cruises, so they put a Pinto engine and automatic in it. But the husband is gone. The son got it running once, a few years ago. It's pretty nice. If I had it, I'd build it like Roth's. But I didn't even ask if it was for sale. I have enough projects. Besides, I have a strong hunch it isn't.

neighborhood I'm not showing you, such as the guy up the block with the loud 1970 Cuda and 1968 Charger, the other guy around the corner with the clean, lowered, 4-speed 1964 Chevelle on polished five-spokes, or the 1930 A sedan down the block that's so covered with boxes in the garage you can't see it.

One of the cars I'd planned to include was a primered 1934 three-window with a small-block Chevy installed by Pete Eastwood years ago. It was here for 25 years, but the owner said he just shipped it to his property in Arkansas. But when I went by this week, he was unloading an "older restoration" 1927 T pickup in the driveway, with a T coupe under a cover behind it, with who-knows-what inside the old garage behind that. Across the street a lady has a once-primo 1964 XKE Jag coupe sitting in the driveway, chrome wires rusting and bright-red paint fading, that she won't drive or sell. The guy with the two red 1955 Chevys and the white, flamed 1940 coupe recently moved away, as did the guy with the 1953 Stude with the early Cad in it. But a black, flamed 1955 Bel Air two-door post with Moon discs has been sitting under a cover in one driveway for about 10 years. And the reclusive doctor who usually has a new Bentley, Ferrari, or Porsche under car covers in the driveway of his zigzag moderne 1930s house had a real 1932 Auburn boattail speedster in the garage when I stopped and asked a few months ago. And then there's the guy with the fully restored 1956 F-100 and rodded 1960s Mustangs, or the 1956 T-Bird on flat tires in another garage, or…well, take a look at what I found.

As I was riding my bike through the neighborhood many years ago, I spotted the unmistakable form of a 1932 three-window coupe under a car cover in an open garage on a side street up the canyon. Consequently, I met the owner, longtime hot-rodder and midget racer Rich Hart, and I featured the coupe, built by Bob Valenzuela of Pasadena, in a story in the February 1993 issue of Rod & Custom. How time flies. In the meantime, Valenzuela built a roadster to match the coupe, and Rich decided he needed it too. This one has a small B&M blower on the 350 Chevy. About the only time I see Rich drive it is on the weekend of the L.A. Roadster Show. The coupe went down the road to make room for the roadster, but the next thing I saw at Hart's house was a worn, black 1955 T-Bird on a trailer. Turns out this is the one the late Carmen Schroeder (as in Schroeder steering) bought new in 1955. It had been sitting for years, but the Harts fully restored it and it's now Mrs. Hart's concours show car. It's stored at the "race shop" in Burbank. The new one she drives daily is parked next to the roadster in the garage. So, what's in your neighborhood?

If you have my book *How To Paint Your Car on a Budget*, you saw what this 1957 Nomad looked like when it drove up to a house down the street about five years ago. Then it was shiny, but I noted

that the paint was checking and it had a wavy right side, denoting filler. It had a 350/350 and some other upgrades (plus blue shag carpet on the door panels), but it's been sitting in the driveway since, with the tires going flat and the paint peeling off the rusting roof. About a year ago a For Sale sign appeared in the window, so I called. The owner said she'd take $27,500. I said, "No thanks." So it sat and rusted some more. Then, amazingly, it disappeared last week. I assume she sold it, but I'm afraid to ask the price.

This one was another big surprise to me. Nearly 10 years ago, a teenager from about three blocks down the street asked me if I could help him paint the body panels on his Ninja motorcycle, so I did. Seeing my 1956 F-100, he mentioned his dad had one like it in his garage. I'd always look as I drove down the street, but I never saw the backyard garage door open. So it was on my list to check out for this book. Then, coincidentally, as I drove by a couple weeks ago, the door was open and I could see people working on a very shiny pickup inside. Turns out it's a 1958 Chevy stepside, and it's a full-on, show-quality truck with a 383 Chevy with all the billet goodies, air conditioning, killer stereo, and tricked-out undercarriage—the works. The neighbor introduced himself as Charlie, said he'd had the truck in the garage for nine years, and had these people over to detail it because he finally decided to sell it to a friend who'd been bugging him to buy it. That was the first, and apparently last, time I've seen it.

One of the best ways to learn how to do something is to find someone who already knows how to do it well, and observe or learn how that person does it. That's more or less what I'm going to do here. Each of the "Finders" profiled in this chapter has something to say about how to seek and find lost hot rods or custom cars, plus you can learn just by seeing examples of what they've found and how they found it. I didn't have much trouble getting any of them to divulge their secrets, because, simply, there just aren't many secrets to it. What was much harder was to narrow each one down to one or two recent finds to show and discuss, because virtually every person profiled in this chapter could easily be the subject of a whole book. Most of them have been doing this for many years, have found all kinds of vehicles, and have all sorts of stories to tell.

Why did I choose these particular Finders when there are so many involved in this field today? There are two primary reasons. First, they represent a range in age, location, personal interest, and style. Second, not only do these individuals find, buy, and sell lots of vintage or historic hot rods, but each of them is a talented and tireless builder (or rebuilder/restorer) of such cars. Variously, they can weld, assemble, build engines, paint, detail, and even pinstripe. And, besides finding choice pieces to trade, each of them has built several excellent cars just for themselves. In some cases these eventually were sold or traded if the price was too fetching or a new project beckoned, but several of these finders have their own keepers that they've had for decades.

Chapter Three

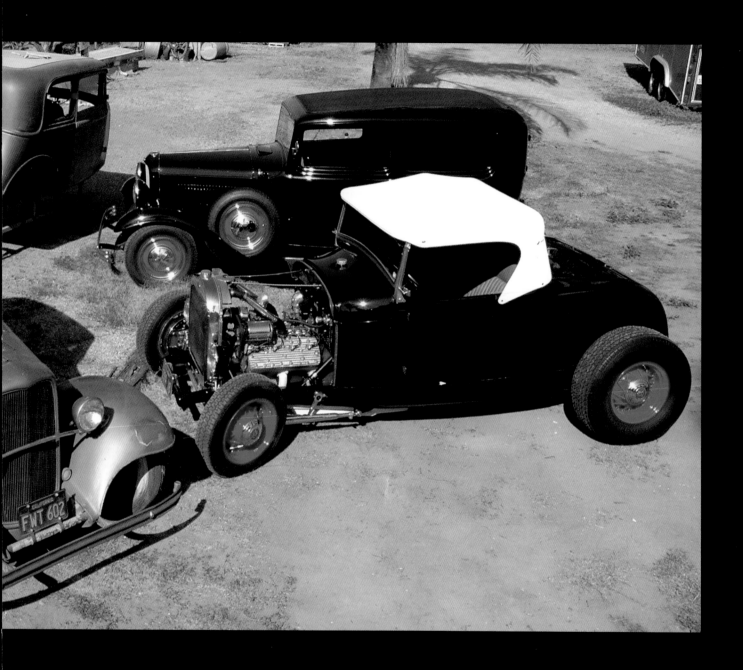

John Koehnke

I met John Koehnke because he was a founding member of the first car club I ever joined, Times Past, in the early 1970s in Santa Ana, California, which is John's home town. He still lives in the same area, which is one of the first clues to finding, tracking, and possibly someday obtaining certain lost hot rods. (By the way, his name is pronounced "kon-key.")

John always built nice street rods, a couple of which I featured in *Street Rodder* magazine at the time. But what really made an impression on me was when he showed up at Lodi or Merced (neither of us can remember for sure) with a beautiful, black, steel-wheeled, OHV Studebaker. It was a V-8-powered, full-fendered 1934 roadster that really sat right and was a killer car. This was my first experience with someone finding a "lost hot rod." It was also John's. The car was built by an early member of the L.A. Roadsters (it still had the plaque on it), but he had quit driving it in

1962. Through a tip from his older brother Bill (who was the real wheeler-dealer of the family), John got it in 1976 or so, cleaned it up, and drove it. Of course, within a couple of years somebody else needed it more than John ... and John had found something new.

Nearly 35 years later, the story's the same. When I asked John how many cars he'd had since then, he gave me a blank look, as if to say, "Are you crazy? I don't know." He'd had the original, time-warp 1935 roadster mild custom seen here three or four years when I photographed it for this book. He had no intention to sell it. But when I went back about a month later to get the early black-and-white photo of it and interview him, he said, "Oh, you're too late. I just sold the car." It turned out I knew the person he sold it to, so I got the photo from him (taken in Seattle in about 1950 or 1951, with side curtains on the 1-inch-chopped folding top, and probably the same Chrysler Butterfly Blue paint). John simply said, "This was the kind of car people hound you to get. People kept hounding me, and I finally said OK." For the right price, of course.

His more general reason for selling it was, "It was keeping me from driving my other cars that I want to drive." One of them is obviously the gorgeous black 1932 hiboy in the photo with John. He's kept this one 18 years. The paint looks great, but up close, the old nitro lacquer looks like El Mirage.

It was first built and painted by an old restorer who brought it from South Dakota when he moved to California in 1956. John says, "He was never going to sell it—never." He filled the door handles and put a good 1939 trans in it (it's still there). But otherwise it was all gennie, including a 1932 V-8.

As for the 1935 Ford, John saw it on eBay. He says he looks at eBay about once a day, but mostly for Whizzer/bike stuff. In fact, the 1935 didn't sell, so he contacted the seller later. The story is: The car belonged to a guy who worked for Boeing in Seattle in the early 1950s, and who brought it with him when he retired to SoCal in 1963. He quit driving it in 1972 and stored it in his garage. Someone in Portland heard about it through a co-worker, bought it, and then put it on eBay. The engine was seized and the top was moth eaten. But nobody bought it. "I had to pay some bucks for it," says John. "I was willing to pay more than anybody else was."

John kept track of it for about 30 years. Then, said John, "He ended up having to sell it. Can't remember why. Needed money for some reason." So John finally got it, built it into this excellent early rod with an Eddie-Meyer-equipped 59-L flathead, and has all the original parts (fenders, lights, wheels, etc.) stored. He's been driving it to local meets for years and says, dead-pan, "I could be buried in it. That would be fine."

The day I took the pictures we drove from John's shop (where he makes and sells Whizzer bike parts— his primary business since 1981) to his house in a black 1940 Ford coupe with a 327 and 4-speed that were installed in 1965. In the shop, among other things, was a once-candy-red, chopped 1932 sedan with 1950s white tuck-and-roll and a 6-71 blown Chrysler Hemi next to a red-primered 1941 Willys Gasser that John recently rebuilt and runs at the Antique Nationals.

Of course the question is why, and the answer is a lesson: "I just really liked the car, the style it was done in. I don't buy anything I don't like." When I suggested he wouldn't buy anything he couldn't resell for more, John replied, "I can't say you'd make money on everything you like. That's not even reality. But I would never buy something I didn't like. It's just common sense to me."

Here are a few more things to learn from John: "The word people use today is 'network.' But you just need to talk to people all the time. The better you are at talking to people, the more you might find out. Patience is a big part, too. If you want something, you keep telling them, 'If you ever want to sell it, let me know.' You have to keep after them, remind them. But this doesn't guarantee a thing. It's still just luck." I pointed out, however, that if you don't ask, you're guaranteed not to get it.

John also mentioned that being local helps. "I've been into cars since grade school. People here know what I have and what I like. They might call me if they find something they can't afford or don't want, but know I do."

Finally, he said, "I like building stuff. Driving your hot rod across the country doesn't interest me in the least. A day trip, sure. I like to drive my cars, a lot. But I'd rather work on them. But not for other people. Let me be quick to point that out."

Have you been taking notes?

Doug Hall

Doug Hall was introduced to me by John Koehnke, sometime in the mid 1970s. He was a transplant to SoCal from Ontario, Canada, and he was definitely into cars, though he preferred early customs more than hot rods. He always seemed to have several of them, though most of us never knew where they came from or, often, where they went. Some he has kept for decades, such as a 1950s-style custom 1956 F-100 that is white, with a chopped top, and lots of powder blue and white tuck-and-roll, including a tonneau cover on the bed with a blue diamond in the middle. Another that he just recently sold, and you may have seen in magazines, is a full-custom 1956 Dodge with canted quad headlights and multi-colored candy-green paint, that is made into a Ranchero-type pickup.

The chopped, channeled, and sectioned very early custom shown here is the one he had the longest. He got it when he first came to California, in the early 1970s, and I was surprised to find out that he had just recently sold it, through a broker, to someone "in Ohio or Pennsylvania who has a big collection with lots of rods and customs." As I say, he's always been a bit nebulous about such things. Likewise,

he got the car through Lynn Williams (aka, C. W. Moss), from "Someone in Pomona who had a huge building full of really top-notch rods and customs, plus some vintage airplanes, who decided he just wanted to collect airplanes and sell all his cars." I can't imagine who that would have been in the early 1970s, and nobody else seems to remember. So this car qualifies as very lost. Nobody knows who built it or owned it originally.

When Doug first got it he lowered it, added the skirts, and did some work on the 1951 Olds engine and 1939 trans. But other than detailing it, it remained unchanged during the 30-plus years he owned and drove it. He thinks the top is a Carson, but it didn't have a tag. He also thinks it could have been built by a coachbuilder such as Bohman and Schwartz in Pasadena.

Further, he conjectures it might be the car shown on page 80 of Don Montgomery's 1994 book, *Hot Rods as They Were: Another Blast from the Past*. The most identifying characteristic is that this is a 1936 Ford Sport Cabriolet, with a sectioned 1940 DeLuxe front end grafted to it. The car in Montgomery's book looks very similar, though its windshield might be chopped

a tad lower, and he states it has "a sunken license plate." Doug's car doesn't. But the one in Montgomery's book is only shown from the front, so I don't know how he'd know the rear plate was "sunken." Granted, the number of sectioned 1936 Ford Cabriolets with 1940 front ends must be quite small, but it's a moot point, because no further ID of the car is given in the book. And now this one is back in a private collection, so we may never see it again.

But this chapter is about "finders," so what's Doug's secret? Well, this isn't one that just anyone can do, but it is effective. For many years, using both single-car and three-car enclosed trailers, Doug worked on a free-lance basis hauling collector cars and other high-end vehicles. One of his regular customers was George Barris, so this tied in nicely with Doug's interest in custom cars. The point is he was dealing with people who owned, collected, or even bought and sold special-interest vehicles. He was bound to come across certain vehicles that might be of special interest to him, and that might also be available, from time to time.

Today he has a fleet of Airstreams and other vintage trailers and camping equipment that he leases for movie and TV productions, plus he's been collecting station wagons—especially mid-1950s Hemi-powered Mopars—because he says that's what is hot right now. However, he's still got a couple of keeper early customs. That won't change.

Mark Moriarity

This chapter presents examples of individuals who have a knack or a system for finding lost rods or customs, and suggests that you can learn from how they do it; that you can do likewise. In this case, I'm not so sure that's the best idea. You might die trying.

Mark Moriarity of Mound, Minnesota, is one of the most talented and energetic people I have encountered in this field. He does all of his own work, in his garage (from welding, to engine building, to fiberglass and sheetmetal fabrication, to paint), and he quips: "I can only have so many cars, space- and money-wise. I live in town." He's not that old (born in 1960), has worked as a self-taught tool-and-die maker for 20 years, and he's found and restored (or built from scratch) an impressive list of cars just in the last 10 to 15 years.

Here's a brief, not-nearly-complete rundown. He bought his first car with paper-route money—a 1955 Chevy two-door hardtop, for $40—when he was 12. By 1982 he drove it as a mild custom to his first KKOA Nats, and kept it until 10 years ago. He also read and absorbed early car magazines. "I was always inspired to own a famous-built custom. But I didn't think I'd ever be able to pull it off," he says today. Then, in 1995, he saw a couple-months'-old ad in *Hemmings* for Roth's *Rotar* air car in black primer. It wasn't the type of custom he had dreamed about—it wasn't even really a car. "I admittedly didn't know that much about Roth stuff at that point. But it was a famous vehicle. I thought it would be interesting. And I could afford it." So he bought it for less than the asking price, fully restored it, and entered it in a big indoor show in St. Paul in 1996, where Roth was showing his *Beatnik Bandit II*. That's where Mark met Ed, and they became good friends. It also started Mark on a tangent of finding and restoring Roth vehicles, as well as building his own fiberglass bubble-top creations (*The Futurian*) or clones (*The Outlaw*).

The next Roth car he found, after seeing a couple reader-sent photos I ran in "Roddin'" in the October 1995 *Rod & Custom*, was the *Road Agent*. The item said it was at O'Brien's Classic Cars in Orlando, Florida, going for $20,000. Knowing it was crazy, he borrowed some money, drove down there, and bought it. After fully restoring it, getting it running, and even driving it to a couple of events, he ultimately sold it to Ralph Whitworth for his museum in Winnemucca, Nevada, which created a relationship that led to several more search-find-restore projects, as well as helping Ralph acquire significant vehicles for his collection.

Mark says, "Once you get known as a guy who likes a certain kind of stuff, your phone rings. A lot of this stuff has found me." Mark was soon part of a network of Midwest collectors/traders that includes Dave Shuten, Larry Tarantolo, Mark Estrin, and a few others who have a knack for finding where "stuff" is and keeping track of it.

This brings us to *Trendero*, the full-custom 1957 Ranchero pickup that was built by Dave Puhl and Johnny Malik at the latter's Trend Custom shop in Lyons, Illinois (on the west side of Chicago), in 1960 and featured in rich pearl yellow on the January 1961 cover of *Car Craft*. Back in the summer of 1982, when I was freelancing, I took a trip to the Midwest to cover the Kustom Kemps Nats in Des Moines, Iowa, but I spent a couple days in the Chicago area at the invitation of the late Miles Masa.

Besides photographing a couple of chopped Mercs he had built, Miles took me on a whirlwind tour of shops, garages, and even streets where he knew old customs were parked or stashed. The most amazing, by far, was what we found after peeling back dusty sheets of plastic in the rear corner of the still-operating Trend Automotive shop. What I saw is what's shown in the black-and-white photos—the nearly perfectly preserved *Trendero*, down to the fully chromed chassis and injected Lincoln engine, the Stewart-Warner gauges in the firewall, the tuck-and-roll, and even the booze bottles in the bed. It was like finding the mummy in the tomb in the middle of the pyramid, and it was certainly a seed for eventually doing this book. Whether you care for this particular

JANUARY 1962 35¢

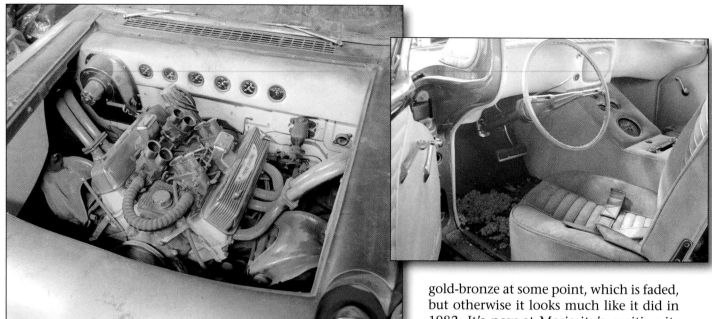

vehicle or not (some do, some don't), you have to admit this was an ultimate lost custom car.

We covered it back up with the plastic and left. The photos were not seen until 1989, and then I said, "It's probably still sitting right there." It was. In fact it stayed right there another dozen years after that, until Malik finally decided to close the business, claimed to "retire" to Florida, and opened a Harley-Davidson dealership there. He took *Trendero* with him. That's where Larry Tarantolo, who's into Harley stuff, saw it and told Moriarity about it three or four years ago. That's networking.

The recent photo shows how it looked as it was being transported, along with Tarantolo's Dan Woods *Milk Truck*, while both were in as-found (though cleaned-up) condition. *Trendero* had been painted

gold-bronze at some point, which is faded, but otherwise it looks much like it did in 1982. It's now at Moriarity's, waiting its turn for restoration (in pearl yellow), as Mark recovers from the full rebuild he just did on the Cushenberry *Car Craft* Dream Rod, as detailed in the January 2010 issue of *Rod & Custom*. When redone, *Trendero* looks to be as nice as the blue Chevy.

The blue Chevy is *Miss Elegance,* first built by Paul Savelesky of Seattle, Washington, in white, with vertical quad headlights, inverted Chrysler taillights, and 1958 Ford side trim, as seen in *Rod & Custom* in 1959 or 1960. Paul then rebuilt the car as seen here to compete at the 1962 World's Fair, with a new front end, candy-blue paint, a fully chromed 1959 Buick engine, and an array of electrical wizardry. There was a mini TV in the dash, a tape recorder in the package tray, and bucket seats that swivel as the doors are opened or closed. In this form it was featured again in *Rod & Custom* and in the May 1963 *Hot Rod* as the "Automated Custom."

Mark remembered it well from studying those old magazines. "There is an image of that car burned in my head. Never in my wildest dreams did I think I'd get to own it." But Mark happened to see it on eBay. "I don't follow eBay religiously. I just stumbled on it." He thinks he was looking at "Custom Cars," and narrowing his search to older models when he saw it. He was the highest bidder, but didn't meet the reserve, so he contacted the owner later to make a deal.

That turned out to be Savelesky's widow. Paul sold the car in 1965 to someone in Canada when he got married. He somehow found it, pretty much original except for Tangerine Metalflake paint, and bought it back in 1998. With the help of bodyman/painter Pete Folsom, he redid the car as you see it here, completing it in 2004 or 2005 in time to enjoy his efforts before succumbing to cancer in 2007.

When Mark got the car all it needed were correct wheels and tires, which was easy, and the right TV and radio, which were much harder to find. Paul had rebuilt the engine, but everything else, including all the pearl white tuck-and-roll under the electrically operated trunk and hood as well as in the cockpit, is from 1962. While Mark's garage (and his den and living room!) can only hold so many cars, and he's had to sell several to make way for others, he says emphatically, "I see this car as a keeper. I love it. I want to keep it forever." I think this time he means it.

Dave Shuten

Dave is a youngster in this group, having been born in 1972. And he more-or-less burst into prominence as the primary restorer (with a team of luminaries) of the Roth *Orbitron* for Beau Boeckmann at Galpin Motor Sports. The finding of that car on the sidewalk in front of a sex shop in Mexico, after all these decades, is the lost rod story of the century, but I am not including it in this book because it has been very fully told (by me in *Hot Rod* magazine, as well as by many others in every other magazine).

Likewise, Dave is best known for his unreal duplication of the truly lost Roth twin-engine *Mysterion*, followed by his own bubble-top creation, *The Astro Sled*, and more recently his finding and restoration of Dan Woods' *Ice Truck* and *Milk Truck*, all of which have been featured on the covers of, and fully documented in, several recent car magazines. So I don't need to retell those stories here (other than to report that *Milk Truck* was done for Larry Tarantolo, for whom Dave is currently restoring the original *Hot Rod Lincoln,* as shown previously, and *Ice Truck* is now "Sitting in some billionaire's living room in Colorado.").

I'm showing Dave's fairly recently acquired, mild-custom 1959 Impala here because it shows a different dimension of Dave's taste and the story of its history and finding is even more interesting.

Dave is obviously and admittedly a child of the 1970s, so his love of the flamboyant show cars of that era is very understandable. As you might expect, he also grew up with Hot Wheels and "Hundreds of model cars that I built and then destroyed." But, growing up in the area of Grand Rapids, Michigan (he currently lives on 5 acres with a large heated shop in Dorr), he started building the usual—well, not exactly usual—muscle cars in his parents' driveway when he was 15 or so.

His first outdoor paint job with a $100 compressor and gun was lamentable, but he kept learning by trying and doing everything himself, which he still does. "I'd build one, then sell it. Then I would build the next one. I couldn't afford to keep one and build another. But I've always loved building them more than keeping them." That has been Dave's mantra all along.

Speaking of unusual, by 1998 Dave had built, on a bet from a friend that he couldn't, a very rumpy Chev big-block 427-powered AMX. It was nicely finished in bright green with black stripes; he took it to the Auburn auction where it sold in 40 minutes. This introduced him to the world of fast-paced, high-stakes, specialty-car selling. It also introduced him to a local network of people in that world that included Mark Moriarity, Steve Estrin, Larry Tarantolo, and a few others. In fact it was from Moriarity that Dave inherited the already crudely begun (by someone else) *Mysterion* clone, and Mark also figures in the 1959 Chevy shown here.

But I'm getting ahead. In high school and college Dave studied art and graphic design. However, he then spent 15 years working as a tool-maker for GM, until about a year ago, when it closed the third plant he had worked at. This was actually timely, because now he can devote his full time to finding and restoring his favorite lost cars. He cites *Deora* and *Lil'* *Coffin* as his "two most inspirational cars," and says, further, "I'm so happy playing with history. That's what I like to do now." He emphasizes that he'd much rather find and/or build cars for himself (and then sell them to build others), and that he'd rather restore real "found" cars: "As Roth said, once they're found, they'll never be lost again." Dave has also been

an inveterate collector of vintage hot rod parts and paraphernalia, saying that he's a swap-meet junkie and he'll never pass up a local garage sale "if it's at an old house or farm."

I've included a photo of just one corner of Dave's large shop, showing a few of the goodies he's collected over the years and uses in his restoration projects. Finally, I note that Dave has developed and combined a broad set of talents that includes studying art and design, building cars in the home driveway, and working at a job requiring machining and mechanical design skills. When I asked Dave how he learned to pinstripe, he casually replied, "Oh, I picked that up in the last couple of years. I think that sort of thing you either can or can't do." Dave not only duplicated Roth's striping on *Orbitron*, but he did the lavender pearl paint, the purple fogging, the lettering, and the striping on *Milk Truck*. Further, to emphasize this blend of artistic and mechanical creation, he said, "The *Mysterion* [clone] was more of an art project than a car project, for me."

Okay, how about this very-tasty 1959 Chevy Impala hardtop? First I should mention that besides 1960s–1970s muscle cars, Dave has built several 1950s customs (he's built *a lot* of cars), including four or five chopped Mercs. Second, remember what John Koehnke said earlier about buying cars that you like? And then add what most have said about having to sell one car to allow buying another. So, this car came from Mark Moriarity, who happened upon it on eBay, loved it, and bought it from a guy who had it in Texas. Then Dave happened to see the car at Mark's, and totally fell in love with it, just about the time Mark came across the blue 1955 Chevy featured previously. Thus, Dave was able to acquire the 1959.

But here's the car's amazing story, according to Mark and Dave.

It was built by someone, whose name has been lost in the shuffle, in South Dakota in 1962–1963. The guy did all his own work, except the upholstery (which was done by a friend who was a fireman and did it on the side), and the car apparently evolved through different paint jobs (starting with pearl white) as modifications continued. It was an original 348 Tri-Power, solid-lifter, 3-speed car that currently has 37,000 miles on it. Besides frenching the headlights, taillights, and nostrils in the hood, the owner chromed everything from the radiator to the hood hinges, added a 4-speed with a console, floor shift, bucket seats from a 1963 SS Impala, and upholstered everything including the trunk, under the hood, and even the wheelwells (which have been lost). The final paint was Buick Lido Lavender Metallic lacquer, which is still on it now.

As the car evolved, the owner entered it in local shows and won awards, so he decided to trailer it to a big indoor show in Denver to see what it would do. On the way the car came loose in the trailer and hit the wheelwells on both sides. If you look very closely in the rear-angle photo you can barely see a chip in the paint in front of the back wheel. Having done all the work on the car himself, he could have easily fixed it. But, supposedly, this made him so mad he took the car home, put it in the garage (or built a garage around it), and nailed the door shut. It sat there for 40 years. Then, in their old age (this would be around 2003 or 2004), the guy decided to sell the car so he and his wife could travel. I don't know how he advertised it, but he made a deal with someone in Texas to buy it. However, according to Dave's version, the week before the deal was done, the guy's wife passed away. But he decided to go through with the sale anyway. Since acquiring the car from Mark, Dave has tried to contact the original builder, without luck, so he assumes he has probably passed away, as well.

But the car exists just as originally built in 1963. Dave says it drives just like a new car and everything works, from the AM radio to the clock. But will he keep it? "I would have a hard time selling this car," says Dave. "It's the only one I've ever bought done. When I saw it at Mark's, I told him I really wanted that car. He had just found the blue 1955 and had to sell this one. So we're both pretty happy. He really misses this one, though."

Alex "Axel" Idzardi

Axel is probably best known as a founding member of the Shifters, one of the original traditional or retro rod clubs in 1992 that are so prevalent today. The Shifters are also well known for their rods-and-rockabilly show, "Viva Las Vegas," held annually in that city. In conjunction with that, Alex and his wife, Celeste, have made a business of organizing and promoting other shows from their home-base in Riverside, California. But Axel has also been buying and selling "found" cars since he was in high school. He comes by all of this naturally. His dad and two uncles drove new, 4-speed GTOs in the mid 1960s. Plus, Alex's father played in rock-and-roll bands and worked as a DJ most of his life. He still spins the oldies today and is an inveterate vinyl, record collector, which leads him to prowling garage sales every week. (More on this later.)

When Alex was in high school (class of 1986) in rural Riverside County, he bought, fixed up, and sold two GTOs. He learned body and paint work in a well-equipped shop class, and has even maintained connections with the teacher, who lets him use the spray booth on occasion. This, you might remember, was the height of a muscle car "bubble" fueled by baby boomers with money to spend on their high school dream cars. Alex found that such cars, in raw to good original condition, were quite obtainable in his area if you knew where and how to look. Not only did he spend lots of time prowling rural areas, back alleys, and older neighborhoods, but he also found out you could get the local Thursday auto-trader-type magazine on Wednesday night if you went to printer. So he did. One other big secret? He prowled mobile home parks. People there are older, don't buy new cars, and they don't have enclosed garages so you can see what's there. You might find some early rods or customs this way, but not so likely.

Alex started out finding, fixing up, and selling muscle cars. Then, when the Shifters first formed (one of the members was Axel's brother Marky), their focus was on "Model As, '32s, and '34s; nothing else existed." So one day when Marky was driving through the family's small home town in the rural, blue-collar suburbs of Riverside, and happened to see an old car with a ribbed front bumper and molded bodywork in an open garage, he stopped to check it out. The owner (who didn't really know what it was, other than an old 1938 Ford custom) said he might sell it, but it wasn't what the Shifters were into—1938 Fords were about the least desirable of all—so he made a mental note of where it was and otherwise passed. This was around 1997.

But early chopped-top customs were beginning to become part of the retro-rod scene soon after that and at least one Shifters member, Kevin Sledge, was into them.

Here comes the unreal part (and lesson) of this story. Earlier I mentioned that Alex's dad went to garage sales looking for old rock-and-roll records. Now in their retirement years, both his mom and dad have made a second business out of buying and selling antiques, as well as records, and they hit all the garage sales within a certain radius every week. Well, four or five years ago, they went to this sale in their own neighborhood (less than 3 miles from their house), and there was this old chopped, custom 1938 Ford with a Packard grille sitting in the garage next to a 1955 T-Bird. Alex's dad, who had bought and sold a

few cars this way, such as Mustangs and such, was eyeing the T-Bird, but the guy wanted too much. Mrs. Idzardi, however, for no explainable reason, flipped at the sight of the old custom. She loved it. The price was right, so she immediately put a deposit on it (lesson No. 2), and said they'd be back the next day. Of course this was the car Marky had seen and ignored several years before.

But when the Idzardis got it home, all the Shifters came over to look at it, and Kevin immediately surmised it was a 1940s custom, from clues like the Packard grille, molded rear fenders, and especially the wide "sunken" rear license plate. It wasn't a famous or magazine-cover car, but Kevin said, "I've seen that car somewhere." One significant clue was what appeared to be 1937 Chevy hood side panels reshaped to fit the Ford. So they went to Alex's house to search through his sizable library, and they found it in the second book they pulled, *Barris Kustom Techniques of the 50's, Vol. I*, on page 10. Shown in white primer outside Barris' Compton Avenue shop in the late 1940s, it was a little-known Barris car belonging to Dick Fowler of Lynwood.

After much more research, Alex found photos in three or four more early magazines, including a couple showing a shiny, dark paint job. So Alex contacted George Barris, who said he remembered the car and the fact that Fowler helped sand and prep it (which was typical). He couldn't remember what color it was, but it was not black. George and his son Brett even came out to Alex's house later to see the car, and sent Alex an official letter of authenticity.

How about that—a real, early, very rare, and very lost Barris custom found at a garage sale! Remember I mentioned earlier how this could work? Even after much research, Alex couldn't learn much more about it. He was told that Fowler was a good friend of Nick Matranga's, and that the car was finished in paint and upholstery, but that's about all. Sometime in the 1960s it ended up in Sunland, northeast of L.A., where it sat until 1979. That's when the last owner saw it advertised in an auto-trader-type magazine as an "old custom" and bought it. Not knowing or caring about the car's history, he pulled the body off and sandblasted and painted the frame, then reinstalled it, along with a small-block Chevy drivetrain and front disc brakes. But that's as far as he got, before Mrs. Idzardi saw it.

So what about the blue coupe that's between it and the two vintage Pontiac engines in Alex's garage?

Well, it's a 1936 three-window coupe. The father-in-law of another Shifter member, Jeff Vodden, was at a garage sale in the older area of Whittier, California, one day and saw a 1930s metal spare-tire cover on the ground. When he inquired about it, the old guy selling the stuff said, "The rest of the car's in the garage." They went back to look, and it was covered with boxes and suitcases, but it was an older mild custom with an 8BA flathead, C-notched rear frame, old blue-and-white tuck-and-roll, and the pink slip. It had last run in 1962.

The guy agreed to sell it for $1,500, and Alex traded Jeff's father-in-law a 1949 Merc for it. Alex "blew it apart," straightened and painted it blue suede, got it running, and then took it down to Tijuana for a full new blue-and-white T&R job for $600. But that's another story for another time.

Billy Belmont

Billy Belmont is the vintage hot rod and custom parts maven of the Northeast, if not the whole United States. Looking for a Latham blower for a Y-Block Ford engine, or maybe a 1953 Pontiac grille for your sled? Call Belmont's Rod & Custom in Dedham, Massachusetts. If he doesn't have it, he'll know where to get it.

Now, Billy doesn't trade in complete cars, per se. But where do vintage rod and custom parts come from? Yes, they usually come off vintage rods and customs. If you find one, you're very likely to find the other. And if you trade in such parts every day, and you've been doing it in the same place for decades, you're going to come across plenty of lost rods and customs, whether you're in the market to buy them or not. Obviously, someone like Billy has plenty of contacts and connections all over the world; he knows who to call for specific parts, and plenty of people call

him, often out of the blue, wanting to sell or trade who-knows-what.

So what does Billy recommend as the best place to shop for this stuff? Swap meets. And (though I have to question his arithmetic) he offers the following as his top-10 favorites in the Northeast:

- Ford V-8 Club at Fitchburg Airport; end of April
- Connecticut Street Rod Association Meet; Bristol, Connecticut, April and November
- Mansfield, Massachusetts, Mother's Day annual meet at Comcast Center
- Englishtown, New Jersey, Raceway; spring and fall
- Ty-Rods meet at Stafford, Connecticut, Speedway; spring and fall
- Thompson, Connecticut, Speedway swap; November
- Rochester, Massachusetts, Gathering of the Faithful swap

All that said, you might wonder what Billy has actually acquired, in the way of complete cars, for his own garage. Besides the blown big-block-Ford-powered '32 Ford hiboy roadster he's had for decades, his most prized possession is none other than the famous *Jade Idol* Gene Winfield crafted from a 1956 Mercury for Leroy Kemmerer in 1959. This is, hands down, one of the all-time best custom cars ever, both being a total ground-breaker when it was built, and never truly equaled since. Think of typical 1950s customs, then look at this car. Not only does it not have a chopped top, but it doesn't have fender skirts, spotlights, sidepipes, or any other add-ons. Using then-futuristic finned quarters from a 1959 Chrysler and hand-forming the quad-light front, Gene then sprayed it with his very first, breathtaking pearl fade paint job that looked almost like the skin of a shark.

It's a wonder this car has survived. Upon completion, Winfield took it on a national show tour, but it suffered the dreaded towing accident in Texas, crushing the roof. After grafting a new roof on it and repainting it, Gene toured it again but, by 1961, Super Stocks were the thing and customs were out. The history of the *Idol* is very hazy for the next 15 years as it passed through several owners, ending up with a bike/van painter in San Jose in the mid 1970s who *completely* disassembled the car, stripped the body for new paint, and then let it sit behind his shop.

That's where renowned customizer Rod Powell of Salinas, California, found it and convinced a customer to buy it. Fortunately all the pieces were in boxes, but they had a hard time finding the frame, which was under a trash pile. Then Rod had to convince the customer, a Darryl Starbird fan, not to put a bubble top on it. Other than Tru-Spoke wire wheels and hydraulics, Rod talked him into a close restoration. Redone by 1979, it won the radical custom award at the Oakland Roadster Show for a second time. But after a couple more years of showing, it needed repainting, so Rod redid it again to its present form. Bob Page of Sacramento then acquired the car (he also owns the wrecked-and-restored Ron Courtney *X-51* Ford), before Billy was able to buy it from him in the latter 1980s. Since then, Billy has added the correct dual quads to the engine and done several things to make the car really drivable for the first time. And drive it he does, whenever he feels like it and the weather's good.

The other "whatever happened to..." car in Billy's stable is none other than the original *Volksrod*, built as a *Rod & Custom* magazine project by Tom Medley in the early 1970s. Prompted by Tom's how-tos in the magazine (including showing how he stitched his own top and upholstery), several of these were built. This one has fenders, hood, and (fake) radiator hand-made by Jim Babb; a chassis by Kent Fuller; and a 100-hp Gene Berg VW air-cooled engine hiding in the bed in back. It took Billy 20 years to talk Medley out of it (it sat under a tarp in Tom's breezeway as he slowly built his 1940 coupe). But he finally got it in 1990, put the five-spoke mags on it, and has been keeping it in primo condition since then.

Julian Alvarez

Julian's gold Duece coupe could be the centerpiece, the poster boy, for this book. If this isn't the quintessential lost hot rod, I don't know what is. And the best part is that it wasn't found in a barn in the Midwest. It was found on Main Street in Huntington Beach. I like to call it the "Beach Find." All the well-rusted chrome attests to this. Here's the story.

Julian Alvarez grew up in a very small wood-frame house in the middle of Huntington Beach, California. He was one of 12 children and the youngest of eight brothers, at least two of whom were very into hot rods. Just before Julian graduated from Huntington Beach High in 1960, a new kid, about three years younger, moved to town from somewhere up in the Inglewood area. His family lived on Main Street, just a couple blocks from the high school. Pretty soon this kid, Glen Quinlivan, was seen driving a really nice, gold, chopped, Olds-powered 1932 three-window hot rod. Nobody seems to know where it came from. It just showed up.

It was magazine-quality nice with full tuck-and-roll upholstery, including a white top insert and

running boards, a dash full of S-W gauges, and a filled- and-peaked grille. It also had a louvered hood, a dropped headlight bar with King Bees, 1947 Chevy taillights, chrome reversed wheels, and a complete chrome dropped-axle front end—brakes, shocks, spring, split wishbones, everything. The engine, with three 2s on an Offy intake, was equally chromed and backed by a stout C&O Hydro, as attested to by a decal in the window. Even the rear frame horn covers were chromed.

From what Julian was able to learn, apparently the father had this car built for his son, and most of the work was done at Ansen Automotive. That's all anyone knows. It was seen regularly driving around town for two or three years, but it was never in any shows or magazines. Then it disappeared in 1963.

Why? Julian is succinct: "His dad bought him a new Corvette." For the Stingray, the kid gave the dad the coupe and the dad locked it in the garage. Unfortunately it was close enough to the beach that rust crept in.

Ten years later, Julian and his rodder brother Andy were chiding each other, Julian saying, "You've got five-windows, but they're a dime a dozen. Deuce three-windows are better, and I know where one is."

In fact, it was two blocks from Andy's house, but Andy had forgotten about it. So Julian called Glen, and Glen said, "Yeah, my dad's got it in the garage. Let's call him. He always liked you. He'd probably sell it."

So Julian called the dad, who said, "Come on over and we'll talk."

I asked Julian how he knew the dad, and Julian said, "He owned the bowling alley in town, where me and my buddies hung out, playing pool and bowling and stuff." If you know Julian, you know he knew everybody in town, and they all liked him. He's that kind of guy.

So Julian, the dad, and the mom sat down at the kitchen table with a pitcher of iced tea, and the dad says, "I've got three grandkids now. Give me $500 for each of them, and the coupe is yours. Here's the pink slip. Except there's one thing. There's a 1959 Olds in the backyard, and you have to take that first. Pay me for the coupe when you can." That's how Julian got this absolutely righteous and otherwise unknown 1932 three-window in 1973, and has kept it ever since.

But, as you can see by what's in the photos, it's not all he has, by a long shot. Let me tell another quick story.

Remember I mentioned telephone linemen, meter readers, and so on? As you can imagine,

Julian's been doing this since he was a teen. It's no big secret, but he says the key is knowing people and tracking stuff. Plus, he's worked all his life doing color-sand/rub-out work, and detailing cars for shops and for collectors of high-end cars. All these people know Julian is into 1932 Fords in particular and old hot rods in general, so several of his cars have "come to him."

The 1929 roadster you see here is, yes, the Bud Bryan *Rod & Custom* project car that helped launch the entire so-called traditional rod movement. After it got rear-ended on the street Bud sold it, someone else fixed it, and then it ended up with a collector in Newport Beach who was more into Ferraris. Julian detailed his cars, regularly. So one day the guy says, "You ought to have this hot rod." Julian wasn't looking to buy it, but the price was right, and he knew its significance. He's taken very good care of it ever since, even if the paint is wearing thin after all the rubbing he's done on it.

That's pretty much how Julian got his completely original, patina'd B400 and the shiny sedan delivery. They both came out of a collection in Iowa in the late 1960s or early 1970s, and went to different collectors in SoCal that Julian knew. He got the super-rare B400 in 1973 when its owner needed cash to start a business. He got the equally rare, original delivery about ten years ago when its owner, another collector whose cars Julian detailed, decided he didn't really want it but knew Julian did. The price wasn't cheap, but he let Jules make payments. Julian put the bright Kelseys on it and had Art Chrisman freshen up the 296-inch flathead. It's sweet. The way Julian puts it, "It's knowing where they're at, and having access." That sums it up.

Julian has a million cousins. "One of my cousins was putting in a service line in Long Beach, down by the circle, and he told me he saw this three-window coupe in a backyard, sitting under a tree. It took me a while to find it, but I did. Except I could never find the owner at home. I kept checking. But you could barely see part of the roof from the street, so I climbed over his fence and put a tarp over it and strapped it down. I didn't want anybody to see it. Finally, one day I saw him mowing his lawn, stopped, and said, 'I want to buy your car.' The guy looks at me kind of funny and says, 'Are you the one that's been leaving me all this produce on my front porch?' I'd been leaving him strawberries, tomatoes, goodies like that [then grown in the Huntington area]. I said, 'Yep.' So he said, 'You know who covered it up?' I said, 'Yep, that was me, bud. I wanted to protect my interest.' So the guy says, 'You really want that car, don't you?' I said, 'Yep.' So he let me have it for $2,500. That was 20, 25 years ago."

And of course he still has it. In fact, Julian has six of them, all in more-or-less complete condition. Another one, with a staggered four-carb Olds with a LaSalle trans, was at his neighbor's house, four doors down. He'd had it since 1955, sitting in the garage, so covered with junk you couldn't see it.

Keepers

Seeking and finding lost hot rods can certainly be fun and sometimes even profitable (though I'm pushing the former, not the latter, angle here). In the next few chapters We'll look at all sorts of rods, customs, and race cars that were the fruitful subjects of concerted searches, were happened-upon more or less by accident, or may very well be lost for all time.

Although I have touched on how certain instantly famous hot rods can burst on the scene and magazine covers, win big awards, then just as quickly seem to disappear, for the most part we're looking for long-lost cars about which rodders ask, "Whatever became of...?" They are the cars that any red-blooded rodder would be thrilled to find covered in cobwebs and dust in the back of a barn, or in a junk-filled garage, after sitting there for decades. We're looking for good-old, forgotten custom vehicles—buried gold and lost treasure.

Well, what about such vehicles that aren't really lost at all, at least not to their owners, who've known where they've been for a good long time—right in their own garages?

Once again, such rods run the gamut from dusty relics that drove the streets or ran the lakes back in the day but were then put away, possibly for a long rebuild; to beautifully preserved one-time show winners that look as good today as they did in the 1960s; and to others that have been built, maintained, possibly rebuilt, and driven on a regular basis for decades. A couple of these cars won big trophies or were featured in magazines years ago. A couple others seem to never get done or redone. One or two are historic for a single detail, such as original Von Dutch pinstriping.

The common thread here is that each of these cars is very cool in its own right, and a couple could certainly be considered famous, but all of them have been in the possession of the same owner—in virtually all cases, that means the same original builder—for 30, 40, or even 50 or more years. The public might not be aware of most of them. Two or three could be on some rodders' "Whatever became of?" lists. But, to the owners, none of these cars has ever been lost. They've known where they were all along. Now you do too.

Chapter Four

Tom Morris' 1929

The El Mirage photo shows a young, lanky Tom Morris (right) and his buddy Jack Clifford with their near-identical, black 1929 roadsters in 1949. Tom got his roadster in 1947 as a basket case after its former owner, Freddie Luce, was killed in a circle-track race. However, Tom is pretty sure the car was owned by the Spalding Brothers (of cam and ignition fame) before that. I recently interviewed 92-year-old Bill Spalding, who remembered their roadster

having "gauges all across the dash," among other details that would seem to corroborate this. The two friends, members of the Velociteers club, built their cars together from the frames up. The only difference? Jack's was powered by a four-banger, while Tom built a healthy 3/8 by 3/8 1948 Merc V-8 equipped with Sharp

Running five pages with 17 photos, the article gave an ample technical description of the car's construction, so that readers could do likewise.

What's amazing is that, other than the removal of small, chrome cycle fenders (necessitated by the then-new California fender law), and the addition of four rows of louvers in the hood top, the car is nearly identical as it sits in Tom's garage in Claremont, California, today. The engine is untouched, including the Zephyr dual-coil ignition built by Tom. The ivory tuck-and-roll upholstery is in place, in very good shape, along with the 1949 Ford anniversary steering wheel and dash full of curved-glass S-W gauges (out being rebuilt when these photos were taken). Even the wheels and tires are the same. The one other big difference, which to this day Tom can't explain, is why he painted the car red and the grille, engine, and even the wire wheels a gaudy yellow. He wishes he didn't.

But that's not why he parked the car. Although it currently wears 1956 plates with a 1957 registration sticker, Tom said it was around 1954 or 1955 when he decided to go back to school to earn a degree, heading first to Fresno State and then to Cal Poly in San Luis Obispo, where he graduated in 1958 as a mechanical engineer and went to work in the aircraft industry, began raising a family, and so on. More amazing is that he somehow kept the roadster throughout this period, "schlepping it from one place to another, including somebody's chicken coop at one time." As you can probably tell through the dust and the green mung on the chrome, the car is in incredibly good condition today.

Unfortunately, Tom's attention has been diverted by several classic British motorcycles he has collected, a couple of which he has beautifully restored. And, yes, that's a pristine 1929 A coupe and a Triumph TR-3 roadster, parked behind the red one in the garage. However, he did just get the gauges all rebuilt. Now all it needs is a little more work and it could be running, Tom.

heads and three-pot intake and a Potvin Eliminator cam. It didn't hurt that Tom got a job in a chrome shop while the cars were being built. Better yet, Clifford was a pattern-maker, so they made several of the cast-aluminum parts on their cars, such as the headlight stands, and a one-off quick-change center section for the Model A rear end that is under Tom's car today.

Not only did Tom run El Mirage from 1949 to 1951, he also gathered several trophies at the Pomona drags in its early days, turning a respectable 103 mph in the quarter. The car's moment of fame came in November 1953, when it was featured in that month's issue of *Speed Mechanics* magazine. Titled "I Built a Drag Roadster" and bylined "Thomas S. Morris," it was actually written by the notable Griff Borgeson and photographed by Eugene Jaderquist.

Alan Kahan's *Von Dutch'd T*

Von Dutch lamented that the vast majority of his artwork ended up in wrecking yards, and the sad truth is that very little true Von Dutch pinstriping exists today—even less from his earlier days, applied to traditional rods or customs. Although it's neither from the 1950s nor flamboyant, the simple, classical-styled apple-green striping on Alan Kahan's 1924 T coupe is one fine existing example of Von Dutch brush work. I'm not saying that Alan's tall T is a lost hot rod, per se, but the original Von Dutch striping on it qualifies as lost art. Plus, the fact that Alan has owned this T since 1958 certainly qualifies it to be included in this chapter on "Keepers."

In fact, the body of Alan's T was rescued from the desert as true vintage tin by his scout master when young Alan was a boy scout. By the time he graduated from Van Nuys High School in 1958, Alan was able to buy the body, a 1932 frame, a 303-ci Olds engine and a Cad LaSalle trans from him, but it was four years before he got the car together, using a much-modified Model A frame and stretching the front of it 6½ inches to fit the Olds mill. By 1963 he got the car painted black, including a set of original fenders stretched to fit and painted black by Dick Korkes at Barris' shop.

Next came a stint in the Navy, during which Alan decided he needed to have the car striped by Von Dutch. When he got home in 1966 it took some doing to find him, but at that time Dutch was working out of his garage in Reseda, with surfboards (among much else) hanging on the walls, and where he was famously photographed striping at least one naked lady.

Alan made an appointment and drove up on a Saturday morning with his wife, who was eight months pregnant. When they got there at 9 o'clock, Dutch asked, "What kind of striping do you want?" Alan asked, "What do you think, Dutch?" He replied "We should do it like an old car." The car had the apple-green Kelsey wire wheels, so they decided the color should match, and Dutch mixed it. Alan said it took him all day, from 9 to 3 o'clock, with Dutch drinking beer or wine the whole time. This didn't even include the hood, which wasn't made yet. The last thing Dutch did, and he climbed up on the engine to do it, was the cowl vent. It might not show in the photos, but to this day that striping is decidedly crooked—but not sloppy (the corners are perfect). When he finally finished, he said the job was $60. Alan noted that he hadn't signed it, and Dutch announced that was $20 more. Thankfully Alan's wife had $20 in her purse, but that was all the money they had. Though the "66" looks more like "62" today, that signature is still there.

Later that year Alan swapped the Olds for a near-new, 225-hp "A code" 1965 Mustang 289 and C4 trans. You don't usually think of a small-block Ford as a vintage engine, but this one is, down to the very rare cast-iron Cobra exhaust manifolds. It's mated to an open-drive 1940 Ford rear end.

With the narrow Ford engine, Alan could get a custom, lengthened hood made to fit. After it was painted, he took it back to Dutch to get it striped to match the rest of the car. He said Dutch did it on a pair of sawhorses in his backyard, again mixing his own color. The striping on the hood and louvers is perfect, but if you look closely the green doesn't match the rest of the car. Such was Dutch. Since that time late in 1966, Alan has changed nothing on the car, nor does he intend to.

What about that nice, red, 1929 roadster hiding in the background? Alan hasn't had it nearly as long as the T, but it has a storied past of its own that was at least partially told when it was featured on the cover of the October 2002 issue of *Rod & Custom*.

And speaking of *Rod & Custom*, surely you remember the classic issue with Danny Eichstedt's tall-top T-bucket coming straight at you on the cover? That was January 1971, and Alan's tall T was featured on pages 58–59. In that feature, Alan was pictured with his wife and young son Aaron. Yep, the same son who was not quite born when Dutch was striping this T, and who grew up to be a founding member of the well-known Choppers car club, as well as the current art director of *Rod & Custom* magazine. It's something about genes, and art, and growing up with hot rods.

Joe Perez' 1951 Ford

Who knows where or how custom car tuck-and-roll interiors originated? But by the 1950s every hot rodder or customizer in America knew exactly what tuck-and-roll was, and probably wanted some form of it in his or her car. Early practitioners of the art included the Carson Top Shop, Gaylord's, Hall's, Runyon, Sahagon, and others. But by the 1960s, two new names became synonymous with meticulous, perfectly straight custom-interior stitching: Eddie Martinez and Joe Perez.

As both rods and customs entered the show car era, a two-tone pleated interior (usually consisting of white and the dominant color of the car) crafted by one of these guys could actually draw more visual attention than the custom bodywork, the lacquer paint, or the chromed engine. Taken to its ultimate, these interiors came to be known as "sculptured," with hundreds of rows of thin, straight pleats formed into organic, three-dimensional patterns in seats, door panels, headliners, floors, trunks, and sometimes even on the undercarriage of the car.

Of the two, Martinez was probably the better known, working for, or out of, Barris' shop much of the time. However, Perez' work was very highly regarded by certain rod and custom cognoscenti of the 1960s such as Ed Roth, various well-known Early Times car club members, and the die-hard customizers of the later 1960s. To me, Perez was known as "King of the 1-inch Pleat," and I prided myself on being able to recognize his work, especially in simple, black, horseshoe-pattern rod interiors of that time.

Joe figures he did 80 percent of Roth's cars. Plus he had some pretty nice customs of his own. One you might remember was a candy-red 1960 Cadillac with mildly sculptured and smoothed bodywork that sat ground-level on hydraulics with Buick wire wheels. It ended up in the Cars of the Stars Museum and was ultimately acquired by Terry Cook (though now it, too, is lost).

Some might be surprised to learn that both of these guys are still turning out beautiful interiors on a regular basis. As always, Eddie seems to get more magazine coverage. But I kept hearing, through connected sources, that Joe was still working out of his house somewhere on the south side of L.A., as he had for decades, but that he was doing mostly high-end restorations on a somewhat limited basis. Like so many of the cars in this book that were rumored to exist, I sort of considered Joe a lost hot rod upholsterer.

Then, to my surprise just recently, I met Joe and his wife at the grand unveiling of the long-lost Roth *Orbitron* at the Galpin Ford Museum. As part of his meticulously accurate restoration of the car, Beau Boeckmann had "found" Perez and convinced him to re-create the upholstery for the car. That particular interior was not one of his hallmarks but, in talking to Joe, what got my immediate attention was a comment that he still had his mild custom 1951 Ford from high school, and that he had just recently finished redoing it, including one of his signature tuck-and-roll interiors.

I was just beginning to collect material for this book, and knew this car should be in it. So I made an appointment to meet Joe at his house, tucked in a small neighborhood between the 710 freeway and the railroad tracks in a city called Commerce, where he

has lived since 1960. He said he graduated from nearby Huntington Park High School in 1957 and started doing (and learning) custom upholstery with Eddie Martinez at that time, mostly for Barris. But by 1962 he went on his own, first to a shop in El Monte, but soon to the slightly enlarged garage behind his house, where he usually works on one or two cars, at most, at a time. When I arrived, the 1951 was in the driveway, and I was very pleasantly surprised to see how nice it was. I'd certainly never seen it before, and nobody I know ever mentioned he had it.

He got it in 1956. He said he'd rather have gotten a 1956 Bel Air, but this was what he could afford. He paid

a friend's dad $215 for it. It was two-tone blue, and he immediately lowered it, put spotlights on it, and then had Cerny shave the nose and trunk. Within a year he painted the car two-tone green (light top, dark bottom), and admits he put a set of Pep Boys seat covers on it (thus planting a seed to learn to upholster?). With a stock engine with dual pipes, this was his mild custom cruiser for years to come.

But young Joe was ambitious, working several jobs, and acquired a 1949 Merc about the same time (which he also still has, stored in his mother's garage), and then a 1951 Cad 62-Series coupe, which he lowered, dechromed, and painted metallic blue as his "nice" car. It *was* nice—he showed me a picture—riding low on chrome Cad wires with wide whites. But, of course, this one was worth some bucks and he parted with it in 1965.

It was about 12 years ago that he decided to redo the Ford. A friend helped him install a 1974 302 Ford engine and C4 trans, with power rack-and-pinion steering adapted to the stock lowered suspension. The engine compartment is simply detailed in black with chrome valve covers and air cleaner. I assume the 1954 Pontiac grille has

been there for awhile, but next came new paint and chrome. The trunk is, of course, shaved, but it retains stock taillights and other trim. The highlight of the car, of course, is the green-and-white, signature Perez tuck-and-roll interior. I love the headliner, and little details like the Impala steering wheel and the laminated dash knobs. But the interior speaks for itself. Just look.

Russell DeSalvo's 1932 Ford

At the Grand National Roadster Show in Pomona in 2009, there was a whole building filled with cars that had won trophies at former Oakland Roadster Shows through the decades. Many of these cars were well-known and recently restored, but several others had been long lost. A few are included in this book. One car in particular had everybody talking. In fact, the first person I saw when I got to the show was Roy Brizio, and the first thing he said to me was, "Have you seen Russ DeSalvo's '32? It's here, and it looks fantastic!" I had to tell him I didn't know what he was talking about.

Here's the deal: DeSalvo built this car in Pueblo, Colorado, between 1962 and 1965, entered it in a big Denver car show, and only got second in class (due to some questionable judging). But California show promoter Harry Costa was there, loved the car, and invited Russell to bring it to his San Mateo show, expenses

An obviously proud young Russell DeSalvo poses for the Pueblo local newspaper in 1966 with his immaculate Deuce three-window and three trophies, including two Sweepstakes, from that season's show tour. The big-inch Buick engine, with its Hilborn injectors and Vertex mag reflected in the chrome firewall, was impressive and loud, but not practical. Note the white-rubber running boards and how the pearl tuck-and-roll runs from the interior into the trunk. The same magnesium wheels and Firestone racing tires are on the car today. (Russell DeSalvo Collection)

paid. So Russ, then 24 and single, quit his job as an automotive machinist, rented an enclosed trailer, hitched it to the 1964 Ford pickup he had just inherited from his dad, loaded up the beautiful black Deuce, and headed out for San Mateo. It turned out to be a six-month tour of West Coast car shows from Portland, Oregon, down to Los Angeles, with stops in Redding, Sacramento, San Jose, San Mateo, and of course the 10-day Oakland Roadster Show. Not only did he win first in class at all of them, he copped best-in-show Sweepstakes at San Mateo, Best Upholstery or Paint at several, and Best Stock-Bodied Rod at Oakland in 1966.

It was at these shows that Russ made friends with Andy Brizio and his several kids, one of whom was a young Roy. They and many other NorCal rodders remembered this outstanding Deuce. But the kicker is that, even though Eric Rickman talked to him about taking pictures, they never hooked up, and the car was never featured in any magazines of the time. So, like me, if you didn't see it at one of these shows, you wouldn't know the car.

When Russell got back to Pueblo, he entered the Deuce in the big Sabers Car Show in Denver for 1966 and justly won Sweepstakes there. However, he also got a new job as a fleet mechanic for the county of Pueblo (where he worked his way to director in a life-long career), married his college girlfriend, and parked the Deuce in his mother's garage, where it stayed for several years. But let's back up a bit.

Russ got into hot rods early, building a 1940 coupe among others, and was obviously mechanically inclined, machining and building engines as his first job. In 1962, a local circle-track racer was "importing" 1932 coupes from Kansas to make into jalopies, and told Russell about a three-window sitting beside a grain elevator in a little town, which he didn't want because they were harder to see out of on the track. It was all original and cherry, so Russ went and got it for $150—twice what the racer thought it was worth. Russ then took the body straight to Bill Dickey's Paint and Body where they both worked on it after hours for a couple years, getting it good

Russ built this large insulated garage in 1979, and that's where the Deuce has been parked, in the corner on jackstands, ever since. The blue, 292-powered, 1964 Ford pickup is the one his dad bought new, and behind which Russ towed the 1932 to California in 1966. And Russell bought the low-mile, all-gennie 1955 Corvette from his buddy, the original owner, about 12 years ago. He's got good stuff and he knows how to care for it.

For fun, we decided to set the car in its show stance, right in Russ' garage (except we forgot to lay the wheels and tires next to it). The Shelby Ford engine is stock, other than the Vertex mag and hand-built chrome headers. With its front Airheart discs, handmade bucket seats, mag wheels, racing tires, and original body trim, this is a typical street/show rod circa 1962–1965.

enough for nitrocellulose black lacquer, which is still perfect on the car today.

Meanwhile, living at his mother's, Russell started on the chassis in the garage, chroming everything he could and building a bored-out, 426-inch 1962 nailhead Buick engine that he fitted with Hilborn fuel injection. While a 1939 trans with Zephyr gears and a 1940 rear with juice brakes were still considered adequate, Russ added some of the latest hot rod equipment, such as Airheart disc brakes on the Cragar dropped front axle, and a full set of brand-new American magnesium five-spoke wheels. When the body was finally ready to mount on the detailed frame, Russ and Phil Sedita built contemporary high-back bucket seat frames out of conduit and expanded metal. Sedita upholstered these in lots of pearl white narrow tuck-and-roll, which continues from the cab right into the trunk, with no partition, "Like the new Stingray Corvettes," according to Russ. It's no wonder this car won so many Best Interior awards.

It should have won some Best Engine ones, too. But Russ says the injected Buick was hard to start and run and, worse, the injection pump left no room for a fan and the car overheated quickly. So the car sat in his mom's garage. But by 1972, with the birth of their second child, the DeSalvos had moved into a house with a double garage, so Russell could bring the coupe home. He entered it in some local shows, and a representative from Ford approached him about putting the car on national tour with the Ford Custom Car Caravan, which would pay some good money. The only stipulation was that he had to change the engine to a Ford. This was fine with Russ, because it would make the car more drivable. So he found a wrecked 1966 Shelby Mustang, pulled the 270-hp HiPo 289, and installed it with the existing early Ford driveline. Pueblo rod builder Otto Rhodes fabricated the motor mounts as well as the hand-built headers as well as the all-chrome four-muffler exhaust that is on the car today.

It took about six months to complete the swap, but Russell never got back in touch with Ford (I think the Caravan disbanded by then, anyway). In 1979 Russell built his current house, "Starting with the garage first." That is where the black-lacquer three-window has been parked ever since. Other than the engine swap in 1972 (and a change from white to black running boards), absolutely nothing has been changed, touched up, repainted, or refurbished since the car was first finished in 1965. But don't think the car hasn't been driven. Russ takes it out occasionally for a spin, and he said he drove it to the first five or six NSRA Rocky Mountain Nationals held in Pueblo. But when I asked him how many miles are on the odometer, Russ just chuckled and said, "Oh, less than 1,000."

This car is a gem. It's a piece of art. At the 2009 GNRS, out of all the cars in the show, it was awarded the Gray Baskerville Memorial "Soooo Bitchin'!" award. Long may it shine in the DeSalvo garage.

Two Six T Roadsters

Where do I start with this one? Take notes; it gets complicated. First, one theme of this book is wondering, and asking, whatever became of some early rod or custom that you were particularly drawn to, back in the day. You might have seen such a car at a show, at the drags, or on the streets of your home town, but as often as not it was featured in a magazine. Such was the case, for me, with an article featuring a low-slung 1927 T drag roadster titled "Slickest of the Slicks" in the July 1958 issue of *Hot Rod*.

With six sweeping plated exhaust pipes on the right and an equal number of injector stacks on the left of the 12-port Jimmy engine, this car undoubtedly had some influence on my long involvement with inline sixes and eventual ownership of a similar 12-port dragster of that era. But this car truly was slick, with its low, lean profile, its polished mag wheels, its cut-down 1932 grille with a polished insert painted with a weirdo design, and mirror-like lacquer that you could tell was a deep ruby maroon even in the green-tinted "roto" photos.

Well, about 15 years ago as I was looking at that old feature and (again following a theme of this book) I noted that the car's owners, Al Andrade and Jules Carvalho, of San Bernardino, California, had unusual names so I called information. Why not? There was no Andrade, but there was a J. Carvalho in nearby Colton. I called and, yes, it was Jules. But, no, the car wasn't sitting in his garage, intact. And he didn't have the 12-port GMC stored in a corner. The car was long gone and he had no idea where. The only thing I learned was that all the plating on the car was copper, not chrome, and that Jeffries (not Dutch) painted the weirdo design.

Sounds like end of story, right? Nope. And here's another lesson on finding lost cars: the power of the press. In searching for the Carvalho/Andrade car, I had come across some photos of it, so I did a small piece on the car in issue No. 6 of *The Rodder's Journal*, saying how I'd found Jules, but not the car. A few

months later I got a call from well-known San Bernardino–area rod builder Larry Braga saying, "Hey, my buddy Woody has that grille insert hanging on his garage wall." Of course, I went out to Larry's shop to meet Woody, see the piece, and find out how he got it.

It turned out the insert is copper and the one-armed, one-eyed monster on wheels is a direct reference to the owners (Andrade had one arm; Carvalho was blind in one eye). It's painted upside-down of course (why? to make it weirder?), and it's clearly signed "Jeffries 1957." Woody said he bought the car around 1959 and converted it to the street with a Nailhead Buick engine, a stock 1927 windshield, and chrome wheels with Merc caps, He retained the unusual, suicide-mounted 1928 Buick front axle. Unfortunately, nobody knows where the 12-port GMC went.

This is where things get complicated; pay attention. On stands in Braga's shop that day was another 1927 T roadster, also inline-six-powered, freshly painted bright yellow and fitted with a nice track nose

and belly pans. Larry said this car belongs to an older guy named Don Clem of nearby Redlands. It turns out Don has had this car since 1946. His father owned the Dodge/Plymouth/Chrysler dealership in Redlands at the time, so young Don had some bucks. So he out-fitted the lakes/track-style T with all Mopar running gear, including a 1940 Chrysler flathead-six engine and 1936 Dodge trans, rear end, and front axle.

The engine currently wears the custom aluminum head and tubular headers Don had made in 1946, along with three carbs on an Edmunds intake, all now polished and detailed. Further, Don commissioned

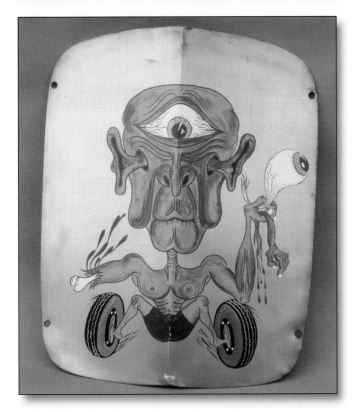

The photo of the car in Braga's shop was taken in 1999, and the unusual thing about it was that Don always wanted the car painted shiny black with red upholstery. So when he finally got it out to finish it, he took it to a painter and told him to paint it black. For some still-unexplained reason, the painter decided the car should be yellow instead, so he painted it bright yellow, as you can see. Not long after this the project apparently stalled again, and I lost track of the car. Braga has since retired and closed his shop, but I asked him recently what became of this roadster. He said Clem got it upholstered (we don't know what color), but didn't wire the car first. As this was being written, he may have just gotten it running once again.

Obviously, this story hasn't ended yet—oh, no. Guess where the Andrade/Carvalho/Woody 1927 T is? It's in Don Clem's garage. At least it was, last time I saw it, about ten years ago, as a bare body and partial frame sitting on the floor. Woody sold the T to one of Clem's sons in the late 1960s, who put mag wheels with big tires on the back and dragster-type wire wheels on the front, with no brakes. He continued to drive it on the street (as you see it in the somewhat fuzzy photo with the sideways 1939 teardrop taillights), as a member of San Bernardino's Early Fords street rod club through the 1970s. At some point he painted the car white, and then disassembled it in the 1980s.

Both of these historied 1927 Ts still reside in the Clem family garage, in one form or another, today. So it goes.

Valley Custom to form the good-looking track nose, full belly pans, and three-piece hood—all of aluminum. In black primer, with no interior, windshield, or headlights (as seen in the photo taken in the alley behind his dad's dealership), this car ran a very respectable 109 mph at El Mirage in 1948. But then it sat, in this form, in Clem's garage for 50 years while he built other hot rods and lakes/drag machines (that's why it's in this chapter).

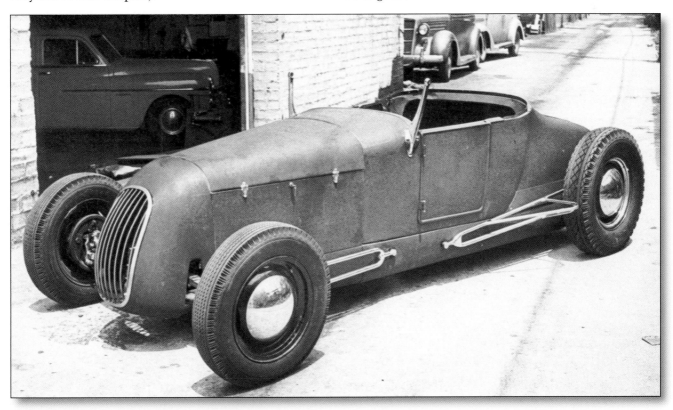

Blaise Vacca's Roadster

The small town of Eagle Rock, California, has always been a hotbed of hot rodding, possibly because Colorado Boulevard ran right through the middle of it, halfway between the Bob's Drive-In in Glendale and the one in Pasadena. This was one of the most popular cruising "drags" in SoCal all through the 1950s and 1960s. It was also the home of Doane Spencer, Dick Skritchfield, Neal East, Paul Chamberlain, and Tony LaMasa (all but Doane being founding members of the L.A. Roadsters), to name a few. But it was LaMasa's little, green, channeled 1932 roadster (later known as "the Ricky Nelson car" for appearing in one episode of the *Ozzie and Harriet* TV show) that was the primary influence on Blaise Vacca, who bought a lot in the Eagle Rock area in 1947 and built his own house there. LaMasa lived about a quarter-mile away, and sometime in the 1950s acquired his low, channeled, fenderless Deuce and started rebuilding it into the green, Dutch-striped, 265 Chevy-powered roadster seen on *Hot Rod* magazine's cover, on TV, and in B movies of the time.

Blaise was bitten by the rod bug, and decided to build something like it. He looked at a few pretty nice stock Deuces,

but decided they weren't nice enough, so he found a totally cherry, stock 1931 A roadster in 1957, and took the body over to Art Fernandez' body shop on Eagle Rock Boulevard (a block away) to make it even cherrier and paint it black lacquer. He also had him cut the floor out and raise it to fit over the 1932 frame he was boxing in the garage himself, with his gas welder. By 1959 the body was on the frame (note the nice lip on the rear-axle cut-out by Fernandez), but the project stalled as Blaise added to the house, raised kids, etc. You know....

Since Tony LaMasa had swapped a Chevy V-8 for the flathead in his car, in 1961 Blaise went to Alan Gwynne Chevrolet and ordered a new Corvette 283 long-block. But before he could get it installed, the 1962 'Vette came out with the new 327, so Blaise went back and traded his 283, still in the crate, for a new F.I. 327, which is in the car today, along with the single 4-barrel intake he bolted on. At that time Blaise also got a close-ratio GM 3-speed trans, and had Cook Machine adapt it to the 1940 rear and torque tube he had installed on the 1932 rear spring.

Now get this: Blaise's son Bob, in whose garage in Eagle Rock the black roadster now sits next to the M&V *Rolling Rice Bowl* (that was re-created for Gray Baskerville, which Bob was able to purchase from Ernie Murashige and is actively running at nostalgia drag meets) says that the cut-down 1932 grille shell on the car came off of John Geraghty's famous *Grasshopper* drag T. Geraghty's shop on Verdugo was also just a few blocks from Blaise's house. Bob says he vividly remembers going over there to get not only the grille—still candy-green with the Dutch lettering and striping on it—as well as the whole chromed front suspension, including an Okie Adams dropped-and-filled axle. Of course they painted the grille black, had a custom brass radiator made to fit, and finished the car off with four small Morris Minor round taillights in the back, chrome-reversed rims

with blackwalls and baby moon hubcaps, a dash-full of S-W gauges, and the good-looking 1-inch rolled black upholstery you see, done by local stitcher Lou Penn.

Blaise enjoyed his channeled roadster for years in this form, loving to race it up and down Angeles Crest highway on weekends, in the mountains behind Eagle Rock. But by the mid 1980s, as Blaise was getting older, street rod components were getting much better, and nostalgic preservation wasn't so important.

Bob and his dad decided to update the car, starting with a TH-350 automatic trans for easier driving, along with a 9-inch rear on coil-overs, four bars and a Super Bell up front, and four-wheel Wilwood disc brakes (and radial tires) for safer runs down the mountain road. In this form (as you see it stored here in Bob's garage), Blaise got to enjoy it several more years before he passed away in 1996.

Though Bob's attention has been focused on the M&V race car lately, he says, "Pop's instructions were that the roadster must stay in the family." In the last month or so he has painted the wheels and grille cream color, got it back on four wheels, and has it running again. Better yet, he says all the parts they took off in the 1980s, including the chrome Okie front axle and the 1940 rear, are stored in his dad's old garage, which is also still in the family. Bob says his son or daughter will inherit the car, and this story will continue.

The Denver Guys

This is another case where trying to find one vintage hot rod turns up two or three. I was going to be spending a day in Denver at artist Darrell Mayabb's, and told him about the book I was doing and the kinds of cars I was looking for. He said I should see Joe Haska, long-time Denver-area rodder and promoter of the big local indoor car show, because he had a nice 1934 coupe that he'd owned since the early 1960s. Great! I called Joe and he enthusiastically said, "Well, if that's what you're looking for, let me call my buddies Bob Marchese and Duane Helms, because they've got cars like that even cooler than mine." I said, "Sure." So Bob picked me up in his red, slammed, flatty-powered 1953 F-100 daily driver and took me

over to his house, with a spacious garage, next to a small lake, on a sunny summer Denver afternoon where the three cars were waiting.

Obviously these cars aren't lost, in the sense of hidden away or gone, because here they are, bright, shiny, and running. But each of these cars has a long history with its owner. One was featured in *Hot Rod* in April 1958. Another was featured in the June 1978 *Street Rodder* in an article written and photographed by the owner of the first car. And the third was pulled out of a woodshed and literally beaten back into the shape of a Model A roadster by its owner 30 years ago. These cars aren't magazine or show queens; they're long-time drivers and keepers.

Bob Marchese's 1932 Three-Window

To see Bob Marchese or hear him talk, you'd never guess he's 74 years old. His name is pronounced "mar-kay-zee," and most hot rodders in the Denver area of any length of time know it. In fact, Bob has probably whittled some parts in his home-garage machine shop for them. He, like Duane Helms, has been a machinist all his life, and it shows in the fine details (which probably won't show here) of their cars.

But, to go back to the early 1950s, Bob was driving a Model A roadster to high school. It was low-buck with a mostly stock four-banger, but at least it had some paint and upholstery and was clean and drivable. So, when he dragged home the scruffy 1932 coupe with the pickup box stuffed in the back (that you see in the fuzzy photo) from a farmer's field in 1953 for $150, right after graduation, his father thought he was nuts. But he wasn't. He was a hot rod-

der. Within two years he had the coupe hammered straight (the farmer gave him the decklid, with four bullet holes in it), got a dropped axle under it with juice brakes, a 1939 top-shift box, and built a 275-inch flathead for it with a brand-new 1953 Merc crank, Weiand heads and three-carb intake, a Weber F5S cam, and a Bill Kenz Lincoln dual-coil ignition. He and a buddy then drove the Deuce, in primer, from Denver to Great Bend, Kansas, for the first NHRA Nationals, and won one round of competition before "Being beat by some guy on a trailer."

When he got home, he turned his attention to getting the now-straight body painted 1955 Ford Sea Sprite Turquoise, with solid hood sides with two rows of small louvers down low, a white top insert and running boards, mild striping, and big and little wide whites on steel wheels with caps and rings (as seen in

the Pete Garramone photo from that era). Bob also had the interior trimmed in black and white, installed a sedan dash so he could mount S-W gauges all across it, and polished and chromed everything on the engine. So by 1958 it earned a well-deserved two-page spread in the roto section of *Hot Rod*.

Despite a couple years in the service, getting married in 1961, starting a family, and so on, Bob drove the beautiful coupe for the next decade and a half, updating things as styles and technology changed. By the mid 1960s, he built a pretty hot Pontiac engine for it, using a 1959 block with a 389 crank, for 366 inches. He got a rare set of NASCAR cast-iron exhaust headers, topped it with three Rochesters on an Offy intake, and backed it with a built-up 4-speed Hydro. But, like so many hot rods that evolved through the 1960s, Bob said driving it was "Like riding a race horse in a parade." And when he drove it to Bandimere to race it on the track, once again he "got beat by some guy on a trailer."

get the 1932 out and redo it, "street rodding" was the new thing and earth tones were in. Thankfully Bob didn't go as far as putting a chrome dog or a luggage rack on it, but it did get stock head- and taillights, cowl lamps, a stock hood, running boards, and even a cap and blue oval on the previously filled grille shell. This time he painted the car tan, with coordinated cloth upholstery, and he even sent the dash to California to be wood-grained by Bob Kennedy. Of course he machined his own narrow and wide Kelsey wires, painted them orange, and had a beltline double stripe added to match.

With the Pontiac somewhat detuned, and having driven the car on the street like this for a few years, it was featured in another two-page spread in *Hot Rod* in January 1989, where Gray Baskerville compared photos from 1958 with similar new ones. But that was 20 years ago! Since then, the best thing Bob has done is adapt a Turbo 350 trans to the early Pontiac block for much smoother street driving. And he's resisting any urges to put the coupe back to its 1958 form, which ironically would make it right in style for today.

So, working full-time as a machinist for the physics research department at a local university, paying a mortgage, raising kids, and doing machining after hours at home for hot rodders, he parked the 1932 in the garage and put a "Don't Ask" sign on it. It sat there for 14 years.

By the time Bob decided to ditch the university job, do prototype machining full-time at home, and

Joe Haska's 1934 Five-Window

Joe Haska, the guy who now puts on the big Rocky Mountain Rod and Custom Car Show in Denver over the four-day Thanksgiving weekend, says he first saw this 1934 coupe for sale on a street corner for $350 in 1959. But by 1963, when he bought it at age 19, he had a hard time talking the owner down to $650. That was all the money he had. It had a shot flathead in it, so he helped a friend install a Chevy in a 1940 Merc to get its engine. Next he drove the 1934 to an uncle's body shop in Kansas, blew it apart, prepped and painted it black lacquer, then drove it back to Denver (in two weeks) to start college. There was a side trip to Vietnam, a couple changes of campus, and a few "driver" vehicles, but he kept the 1934. In fact, he and his wife-to-be went on their first date in it (they've now been married 42 years). They're both keepers.

Because Joe never parked or stored the coupe for any length of time, he kept changing it with the trends, like a typical hot rod. In the mid 1970s he pulled the car apart for another rebuild and repaint, This time, in keeping with 1970s styles, he painted the body maroon with black fenders, swapped in a Ford small-block with the early driveline, and upholstered it in black 'hyde wide rolls with a row of buttons, "early style."

In fact, he and two friends redid their Model 40s together, including a chopped black sedan and a butterscotch-yellow 1933 coupe, that appeared together in a five-page feature in the June 1978 *Street Rodder*, written and photographed by Bob Marchese. With front licenses (made by Joe) reading "Good," "Bad," and "Ugly," the three cars all had stock head- and taillights, cowl lights, full bumpers, and rode on chrome Tru-Spoke wire wheels with the back tires protruding from the fenders—an extra one mounted at the back of each as a spare. Joe said he later reupholstered his car in gray cloth to be more contemporary.

But times change, so, in 1989 he pulled the coupe back down to a bare frame and redid it once more. This time he put a flathead back in it with the existing early driveline, lost the spare tire and bumpers, put 1939 teardrops in the back fenders and punched louvers in the rear pan, and painted the car (himself) all black lacquer once again. Since he was going for the new-again nostalgia look, he put small sealed beams on the front, added hood sides with hot rod

louvers, made his own small nerf bars, and went for big and little wide whites on bright-red steelies, all tucked neatly under the fenders. Finally, to complement the Bell wheel and stick shift inside, he just recently had the interior redone in tasty, traditional black with white pleats (including the headliner), all in real leather. Yes, it's a nice piece, but this show promoter stresses it isn't a show car, it's a driver. And it just might get rebuilt again, after he's had it 50 years, or 60.

Duane Helms' 1929 Roadster

Of these Denver hot rods, Duane Helms' is by far the newest. He's only had it 30 years.

Consequently, Duane has had quite a few other cars, including ten Model As ("because they're cheap"). He got his first at age 14, a pickup that he cut the top off of and made into a roadster. He fitted it with a flathead V-8, but sold it before he could drive in order to buy a better one. The family lived on a farm, but they didn't have welding equipment, so "I used a drill and a hacksaw. Everything was bolted together." Obviously, he learned to be a crafty guy, and eventually spent 40 years working as a machinist in the aircraft industry.

Seeing Duane's Model As, an older neighbor finally mentioned one day that he had one stored in a lean-to out back. When Duane asked what kind it was, the neighbor said, "I don't remember." He thought it might be some kind of coupe with the top cut off. So Duane asked if he could see it, and the neighbor said, "Not really." The problem was that the shed was piled with lumber and other junk, so you literally couldn't see the car.

It took a year and a half before the neighbor would let Duane remove enough of the stuff on top of it to finally see the tops of the A's doors, and ascertain that it was actually a roadster. So he asked the guy, on the spot, how much he wanted for it. He said he'd paid $300 for the car, so that's what he wanted. In 1979 that sounded like a bargain, so Duane paid the money and kept digging. When he finally got the thing out, he realized he might have acted in haste.

Yes, it was a 1929 Model A roadster body, but it was mounted on a 1934 V-8 frame. To do so, they not only cut the floors out, but also cut the rear of the body apart with tin snips and used angle iron and riveted sheetmetal to widen it 3 inches. It had a 1932 shell (the one on the car today), but it was also cut with snips and peeled back to clear the 1934 radiator. And the rest of the body was just as bad. As Duane put it, "For $300, I didn't get a bargain."

But he isn't easily daunted. He carted the mess home and completely disassembled the body. Admitting he's no metal man, he started straightening the panels the best he could, using some plastic filler here and there. But it turned out one of his co-workers was

an old-school body man, and he said, "Bring that stuff to my place and I'll show you how to do it." Well, Duane just watched as the old man used a torch to heat areas the size of a dime, all over every panel, then used a hammer and dolly or just let it shrink on its own. "The metal has a memory," he'd say. And sure enough, after watching this guy do this repeatedly, it started looking just like a Model A body again. Scolding him for using any plastic filler, Duane said the guy used 8 ounces of lead, at most, to finish it. Then, to show how good it was, he painted it black lacquer—the same paint on the car today—and then wouldn't take a penny for all his work. Whew!

Meanwhile, Duane, who is a swap-meet junkie, started looking for a Deuce frame to mount it on, but couldn't find anything decent for an affordable price. But he kept looking at the 1934 frame it came on and decided, using some Model-A front rails he had, he could make his own frame to fit the narrow 1929 body.

Look closely. It's hard to tell that it transitions from 1934 to Model A somewhere around the firewall. Duane said the hardest part was narrowing the 1934 X-member to fit and accept the 1939 trans. The rear is a 1937, which is 2 inches narrower than the A, but the center section is a very early A-V-8 Halibrand (serial number 183) Duane got at the swap meet. The "Divco" 18-inch rear wheels were an extra set from Tommy Thompson's streamliner (from Denver), and Duane got the rare Thickstun PM-7 high-rise dual-carb manifold from someone who wanted a cheap low one in trade. The 239-inch engine has an equally rare Winfield SU-1A cam that

Duane saved from his flathead dragster days many years ago. The stretch-drop front axle came from a swap meet, but Duane made a fixture to fill the ends and re-bore the kingpin bosses. His most recent swap find is the T-33 aircraft seats, which he cut down 2½ inches and made his own tools to re-rivet along the tops.

That's the kind of car this is: a sort of funky, but beautiful, hot rod pieced together bit by bit by a couple of talented, patient, and resourceful craftsmen from a once-cobbled-up piece of junk that was very lost at the bottom of a woodpile.

Lost and Found

This chapter doesn't take much explanation or setup. It's the meat and potatoes of the book. Each of these rods or customs was well-known in its day. With a couple of exceptions, all were featured in magazines, usually on the cover. Most have not been seen by the public in decades. And a few have even been the subjects of concerted searches. The types of cars, their stories, and their present conditions vary widely. But all of them fall into the "Whatever happened to..." category. I think several of them will surprise you.

Chapter Five

Joe Cruces' *Tall T*

his is one I wondered about for years. Obviously, I wasn't the only one taken with the angular, tilted proportions of this somewhat incongruous hot rod. It was featured prominently on the cover of *Hot Rod* magazine (October 1960) when it had a flathead engine, and again on the cover of *Rod & Custom* (October 1962) when it had an Algon injected small-block Chevy, and was accompanied by *Rod & Custom*'s first "How to Build the Model" drawings. Maybe one reason I liked it so much was that I was an avid model-car builder at that time (Aurora made a very popular 1/32 scale kit of it, by another name). Even Ed Roth told builder Joe Cruces that this somewhat cartoonish rod was very influential on him, calling it a "China closet on wheels," largely because of all the tall, flat glass windows. About the only trophy the car didn't win in its fairly brief, regional car show career was the America's Most Beautiful Roadster cup at Oakland, only because it had a top.

This was also one of the last cars I found. When I started researching this subject, *Tall T* was at the top of my list. But nobody had seen it, basically, since 1962 or 1963. Hot rod styles changed very quickly in those days (exemplified by Cruces' switch from flathead to Chevy power). And, after quitting his job at the local Chevy dealers and opening his own custom body shop in his home town of Vacaville, California, Joe turned his attention to building a space-age roadster with a completely hand-formed, Cerise Metalflake body and futuristic single-stick operation, which he dubbed *Crucifier* and entered at Oakland hoping to win the big trophy. It was a top contender, but lost to Bob Reisner's twin-engine, equally futuristic *Invader*. Then Bob Cruces seemed to disappear, too.

I asked all the NorCal rodders I saw, guys like Andy Brizio and Dennis Varni and other Bay Area Roadsters. Nobody knew. Finally, in frustration, I called information for Vacaville, California. There was no Joe, but there was a Frank. I called. It was Joe's brother. He told me Joe had moved up to Chico, about 125 miles north, in 1970, to restore classic cars for a wealthy "rice farmer," who set him up with a full shop and crew. He said Joe was now semi-retired and was planning his 50th wedding anniversary (with the same wife you probably remember from the *Hot Rod* cover, right?). He gave me a home and shop number. I called and got Joe, who said the intact body from *Crucifier* was hanging from the rafters (he had sold the completely chromed chassis long ago), and that he had been doing high-end restorations on cars like 1930s-era Mercedes, Hispano-Suizas, and Duesenbergs ever since. In fact, a 1931 Chrysler

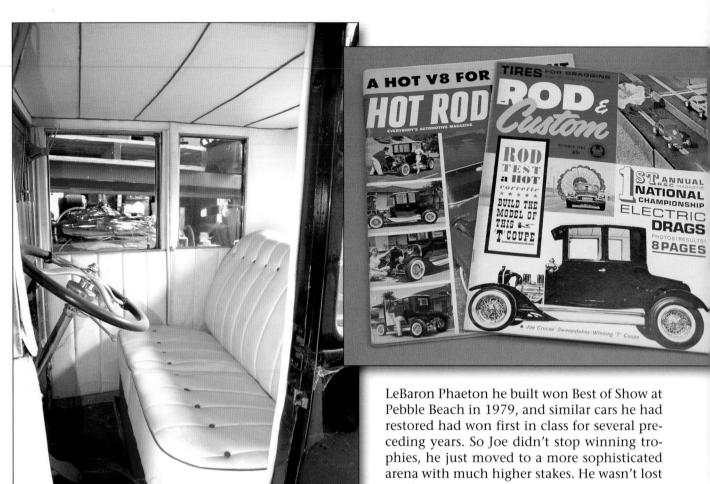

LeBaron Phaeton he built won Best of Show at Pebble Beach in 1979, and similar cars he had restored had won first in class for several preceding years. So Joe didn't stop winning trophies, he just moved to a more sophisticated arena with much higher stakes. He wasn't lost at all.

But where did *Tall T* go? Joe sold the car to Gerald Blair of Monterey in about 1963 to finance the building of *Crucifier*. Blair replaced the injected V-8 with a Chevy II four-cylinder, painted the white frame and red undersides of the fenders black, removed the white-and-red upholstery from the splash aprons, and apparently drove the car in this form for some time (because the red carpet is pretty worn), and then stored it in his barn, less engine.

Enter Claude Bennett, also of Monterey and a friend of Blair's. Bennett first saw the Cruces T at a Modesto car show when he was a young teen and was smitten by it. In fact, he had crawled under the car to admire the chrome chassis and was forcibly removed by two guards who dragged him out by his feet and ejected him. But he never forgot the car. Well, as he was talking with Blair in 1985, Blair said, "I think I'm going to sell my Model T." Bennett asked what T it was. "I couldn't believe it," he said recently. "This was my favorite car, and a guy I'd known for years had it in his barn and I didn't even know!" Needless to say, Bennett bought the car, much as you see it here.

The original lacquer paint, the red-and-white upholstery, and the original chrome are all in decent condition, given the car's age. It would clean up quite well. The red 1939 trans with a chain shifter and skull knob sits in one corner, while a hi-po 283 with complete Algon injection sits on a stand in another. The whitewall Bruce's slicks are gone, but the Buick wires are original. But that's about it. He has stored the car, as is, in various places since he bought it. It's currently in a crowded World War II hangar, under tarps, behind a 1957 T-Bird project. Bennett says it's enough for him just to own it, and maybe climb in and sit on the white tuck-and-roll every now and then.

The Bo Jones T

In the mid 1960s, Bo Jones, then of Van Nuys, California, looked at a poster with an old photo of roadsters at Muroc dry lake in the 1930s, pointed to one in the middle that was a narrowed, tail-less, "Modified" T, and said, "I'm going to build one of those." He had collected a lot of hot rod—and Model T—parts, and he was a crafty guy, so 12 weeks later he had the car finished.

He narrowed a gennie body 8½ inches and had his buddy Willy West bend up a hood and belly pans and punch them full of louvers. He hung a dropped-and-drilled axle on quarter elliptics in front and a Halibrand quick-change with rare Kinmont disc brakes and hand-made friction shocks in back, and powered it with a then-new Chevy II four-cylinder engine and 3-speed trans. Painted bright orange with tall, skinny, red Kelsey wire wheels and big 18-inch truck tires in the back, this simple, little street rod looked totally radical when it appeared on the cover of *Rod & Custom* in October 1968. It's hard, today, to understand how influential this car was at that time, because it has been so widely emulated and downright imitated ever since. It not only set a style for T roadsters that continues today, but it was also one of the very first retro rods to be built.

it to Mike McKennett's shop in Portland, where it was rebuilt, including new paint, chrome for the radiator shell and suspension parts that were red, front disc brakes, an automatic trans, and a few other updates he might not have made if provenance were as important then as it is today.

Next he took the sedan to McKennett's for similar treatment, including a three-piece aluminum hood and chrome Buick wire wheels. Schoonhoven drove, showed, and enjoyed the two Ts this way for years, as seen together on the cover of *Rod & Custom* as late as August 1995. But not long after this, Bob decided to retire, move to a warmer climate, and build that Deuce hiboy he still wanted. Fortunately, Ron Ford demanded first dibs on the sedan if Bob ever sold it, and Roy Brizio, who had loved the Modified since he saw it as a young teen at a Roadster Roundup, had been pestering him to buy that car. Schoonhoven had decided that, if he should sell, they should stay a pair.

Well, it turns out that Ron and Roy are good friends, so they convinced Bob to sell them the cars together, Roy getting the roadster and Ron getting the sedan back again. Better yet, they decided the cars should go to the large building at Ron's car dealership in Vancouver, Ocean Park Ford, where he keeps his 18-car rod collection, which includes a couple of woodies, a couple of Ts, and a couple of well-known Brizio-built cars.

Since acquiring the Ts, they've both been fitted with tall, narrow, red Kelsey wire wheels and appropriate tires. Otherwise, they remain as they were in *Rod & Custom* in 1995. If you happen to be in the Vancouver area and want to see them, Ron said to call the dealership and ask for him, and he'll give you a tour. Or, if it's around the middle of September, and especially if you're driving a traditional hot rod, ask what day Ron's big, annual rod gathering is going to be. It's patterned after Andy's Picnic (as in Brizio), it's a lot of fun, the rod collection is open, and yer'all welcome.

About the same time Bo also built, in about the same number of weeks, a similar 1926 T sedan. He painted it the same orange, with the same red wire wheels, and powered it with the same Chevy four-banger. Besides a hood full of louvers, it also had louvers in the back, just above the quick-change rear and a chrome crossbar with a trailer hitch. Although he drove the Modified plenty, including to the 1960s Roadster Roundups, he also liked to hitch it to the sedan and drive them both into a car show, and just park them, as a pair. What a pair!

But Bo was always on to new projects, his next being a straight-8 1938 Buick coupe (where is *it* today?). So he sold the sedan at the L.A. Roadsters swap to someone from Portland. That's where long-time rod collector Ron Ford from Vancouver, British Columbia, saw it and decided he had to have it. He bought it in 1969, and began driving it to local events. But that's where Pacific Northwest show-promoter and rod-lover Bob Schoonhoven saw it and decided *he* had to have it. It took him until 1974 to convince Ford (in a weak moment) to sell.

Meanwhile, Dick Megugorac knew where the roadster was in pieces, and when Schoonhoven called him about building a Deuce hiboy in the early 1980s, Magoo said, "No, what you need is Bo's roadster to go with the sedan," and brokered the deal. Since the roadster needed to be reassembled anyway, Bob took

The Otto Rhodes F-100

This is one of those cases where the long-lost hot rod has become more and more found since this book project started, but I think it is certainly significant enough to include.

It was very lost for more than 40 years. Like Russell DeSalvo's beautiful 1932 (see Chapter 3), this 1953 F-100 pickup came from Pueblo, Colorado, and Bill Dickey's custom shop, from about the same period. Here's the short story:

When Otto Rhodes graduated from high school he bought the near-new pickup and decided to customize it like a couple he had seen "From Barris' shop" with the front fenders pulled in at an angle, canted quad headlights, an oval grille, and rolled pans with no bumpers. The trouble is that he didn't know how to do such work, so he took the truck to Bill Dickey's, which was known as *the* custom shop in the area. But, since Dickey made his daily income from collision work, he let rod and custom guys bring their projects in and work on them after hours, with Dickey either helping or showing them what to do.

Having seen the restored truck in Pueblo recently, Dickey commented, "Otto didn't know how to weld when we started this truck. So I cut it all apart, and made him weld it all back together." This included chopping the top, which Otto hadn't initially planned to do. Continued Dickey, "Otto didn't know how to do lead. But he started at the bottom of that [front] pan, and by the time he got to the top of the hood, he was a master. I'm not joking."

Together they finished the truck, top to bottom, in white-pearl paint with red Metalflake accents, matching upholstery in white rolls with red, buttoned frieze, and a bored-and-stroked and chromed Olds mill with six carbs. It began winning show trophies everywhere in the region, and was even photographed by local freelancer Tony Spicola for a spread in *Hot Rod* magazine. But then young Otto got drafted and spent two years in Germany in the Army. His truck, which had been photographed in 1960, didn't appear in *Hot Rod* until the July 1962 issue, when Otto was overseas. Telling your Army pals about your full custom pickup back

HOT ROD SHOWCASE.....OTTO RHODES' OLDS-POWERED FORD PICKUP

drive the trophy queen around the local circle track. So when Otto finally got home, he decided he needed to rebuild and upgrade the truck, but do the work in his own garage so he would get the credit. It bothered him that his chassis wasn't chromed, like other cars his truck beat. Plus the six-carb Olds was problematic. So he made an excellent deal with a good chrome shop to trade the Olds engine for plating everything on the undercarriage. Typical of the times, Otto upgraded to a 360 Ford FE big-block engine and a twin I-beam front suspension (for which he had to make his own crossmember), which were the latest options in new Ford pickups by that time. Then he cut the whole dashboard out, intending to make a newer, more futuristic one with a 1965 T-Bird gauge cluster.

home was one thing, but actually showing it to them in *Hot Rod* was something else! Better (if strangely) yet, the next issue showed the truck again, on a full page, in full color, with young Otto and a scantily clad lady standing next to it. This was one of the first two interior color pages ever printed in *Hot Rod*. Why the feature on the truck was a month prior, I can't explain.

Also, while Otto was overseas, Dickey continued to show the truck and even use it to do things like

However (this is where the story begins to sound like so many others in this book), Otto began a career as a welder at the huge steel mill in town, got married in 1966, and had a son a year later. With the chassis complete and the still-pearl-painted body on

the location of that historic color photo in *Hot Rod* magazine turned out to be the site of Tom's high school. It was meant to be.

Tom flew to Pueblo, made a deal with Otto, and conferred on how the truck should be finished. The pearl paint was yellowed and cracked, of course, but the body and lead work were perfect. More amazing, 95 percent of the chrome on the truck was original. The only real question was the interior. Otto didn't like what was in it before, and had sold it all to a friend early on. So he and Tom came up with a 1960s "spacey" theme of swivel bucket seats upholstered in pearl white with red carpet by Howdy Ledbetter. Otto had reworked the firewall, making a panel in the middle surrounded by tubing in the shape of the grille, in which he planned to install frosted plastic with lights behind it to illuminate the engine at shows. That didn't get done, but when Tom viewed the polished engine through the opening in the firewall he thought, "Wow, that looks good. Let's put a window there." So he did, using Plexiglas. It's just one more highlight in this stunning custom F-100.

sawhorses, the truck sat in the garage. And sat. As his son grew older, he thought maybe they'd finish it together, but the son wanted his own pickup, not his dad's. Finally, by age 70, Otto admitted it wasn't going to get done, and mentioned to a long-time friend that he'd consider selling it.

The friend knew a former Pueblan who just might be interested. Tom Pagano had moved to Sacramento, California, in 1995 and started a very successful custom shop with his son, TJ. Tom was more than interested; he was ecstatic. This was the truck that turned him on to customs in the first place, having seen it as a child in a special exhibit at the county fair. It was the first custom vehicle he ever saw. In fact,

After more than 40 years Tom has it back on the show circuit, winning trophies and being featured in magazines. You've probably seen it. It's not lost anymore. And we're all glad it's back.

Ron Aguirre's *X-Sonic* Corvette

Ron Aguirre's Corvette, *X-Sonic*, was one of the first customs with a bubble top. It is also often acknowledged to be the first car to use an aircraft hydraulic suspension, have no steering wheel, and later be completely remote-controlled. And it is one of my favorite cars, period. It is best known for a feature and a small cover photo in the September 1961 *Rod & Custom* when it was a pearl aqua with darker fade outlines as seen in the photo with Ron in the car (taken, incidentally, by Ed Roth). I wish I had better color pictures of it, but I don't. These rare photos came from Aguirre's own albums. I also wish I had room here to show more pictures and relate in greater detail some of the hilarious stories Ron told me about driving this wild, futuristic, bubble-top car on the street. For a fuller account, I refer you to my book, *Ed "Big Daddy" Roth: His Life, Times, Cars and Art* (published by CarTech).

Aguirre's relationship with Roth began as soon as he purchased this Corvette new in 1957. After lowering it as much as possible and adding side pipes and wheelcovers, he took it to Roth at The Crazy Painters for flames and striping. But almost immediately after that he started modifying the fiberglass body himself, first adding vertical quad headlights with an Opel grille in front and fins with custom taillights on the rear fenders. I remember seeing this car at local shows when I was a teen, as well as cruising the drive-ins, and it seemed to have new changes and different paint every time I saw it. In the rear-angle photo taken at a once-only one-day car show at Disneyland, it has scoops in the roof, tuck-and-roll in the coves, and a panel paint job by Roth that only lasted that one day! I don't even know what color it was, but they didn't like it.

The other photo, showing further body modifications, was probably the last taken before Ron and his dad figured out how to "blow" the bubble top for it. Given its extreme rake, this was probably when Ron devised the first hydraulics for the front suspension, using a hand-pumped porto-power. Ron's dad then discovered electrically activated aircraft-landing-gear hydraulic cylinders at a surplus store, and devised a system that would raise and lower the front of the car at the flip of a switch—much to the chagrin of police who tried to ticket the car for being too low. The same system is still being used by lowriders today. The Aguirres also shared what they had learned about hydraulics

and bubble bowing with Ed Roth, who was building the bubble-top, hydraulically steered *Beatnik Bandit* at the time. Ron points out, however, that *X-Sonic* used an electric motor, operated by a toggle switch, to steer. "It was hard to drive on the freeway," he said, "But it worked!"

Roth and Aguirre, in fact, often traveled together as they took their cars to shows around the country in the 1960s. The difference was that Roth built a new car each year, and Aguirre just kept repainting his. Larry Watson (who was also painting Roth's cars by then) says he painted it seven times in the bubble-top version, including what he claims was the first metalflake paint job in California (using gold Metalflake Ron brought back from New York).

But no matter how many times you repaint it, any show car has a limited life span, and *X-Sonic* sadly ended up sitting in Aguirre's back yard, where the bubble soon weathered and cracked and the paint faded away. Ron kept it there for years. But by the early 1990s I was told a car fitting its description, less bubble, engine, and interior, was seen at a Corvette restorer's shop in Whittier. I rushed over and immediately recognized the gray-primered shape. It was missing the grille and taillights, but the full chassis, including most of the hydraulic system, was there. It turned out the restorer had bought it from Aguirre simply as a parts car, not knowing any of its history. I explained the car's significance to him, and showed pictures of its then-condition in the "Roddin'" section of the June 1991 *Rod & Custom*. Realizing that it could be worth some bucks, the owner decided not to dismantle it.

That was nearly 20 years ago. I have no idea how many times it has changed hands, or how many bucks have been spent, but I'm glad to report that it still exists, in the condition you see, in another restorer's shop in Southern California. It's not bad, considering how many paint jobs have been stripped off its highly modified fiberglass body. And the current owner swears he's going to restore it. But so far he's only been storing it. However that, as they say, is better than the alternative.

Gil Ayala's T-Bird

The Ayala brothers, Gil and Al, were the East L.A. equivalents of the Barrises. Their shop (Gil's Auto Body at 4074 E. Olympic Boulevard) unquestionably turned out some of the earliest and best custom cars ever. The only thing they lacked was George's knack for promotion, both of himself and the creations he built. While Barris built cars for movies, TV, and their stars as the days of the classic custom waned, the Ayalas became known for highest-quality metalwork and paint jobs, especially candy-apple red. By the mid-to-latter 1950s, Gil's calling-card vehicle was his own moderately customized, but brilliantly candy-apple-red-painted 1955 Thunderbird, which went through numerous changes but was best known in the finned, scooped, and pinstriped version you see on the cover of *Motor Life* magazine, May 1957.

The somewhat blurry photo of a shirtless Gil rubbing a beautiful new candy job shows the car in its final and cleaner form with the scoop removed from the hood, the less-pronounced headlights, and the gold mesh fins removed from the rear fenders. I'm not sure when this photo was taken. In fact, when I did a two-part story on the Ayalas in *The Rodder's Journal* (Nos. 39, 40; 2008), when Gil and Al were gone, nobody seemed to have any idea of what had become of the well-known T-Bird. It just vanished.

Then, as I was interviewing family members and anyone who knew or worked for the Ayalas, I heard through the grapevine that Dan Cuellar of Norwalk, an avid custom-car enthusiast who drives a gold-scalloped 1956 Chevy and helped to revive the Ayalas' Auto Butchers club from the 1950s, had not only found the T-Bird, but had acquired it. Or, I should say, its remains. He had heard that two guys were parting out a custom 1955 T-Bird and, being an Ayala fan, figured he'd better go see. Yep, amazingly, it was Al's long-lost car. The guys who had it knew nothing of its history (it had L.A. police impound numbers still written on the hood).

It has a small-block Chevy engine partially installed. One door and all the glass is missing. But parts such as the Pontiac bumpers and Lincoln taillights were stashed inside. The body is in gray primer. There is some rust from sitting outside. And you can see that it's banged up. But it is restorable. Dan currently has it stored in a lot, covered in tarps, because he has no garage space at home. He's not sure what to do with it because just buying the carcass stretched his finances slim. But the important thing is that this important custom has been saved by somebody who knows what it is and cares about it.

Roth's *Old Pro* 1929 Pickup

Since I was going to Salt Lake City to see and photograph the Glen Hooker Merc, I called my favorite contact there, longtime rodder and illustrator Mickey Ellis, to ask if there were any other significant lost hot rods or customs in that area. He thought for a minute, then said, "How about Ed Roth's Model A pickup, *Old Pro*?" Sure! Well, small world that it is, wouldn't you know that Gordy Brown (current owner of the Glenn Hooker Merc, see page 102) was heavily involved in this vehicle, too?

Unfortunately, it turned out that Mike Carson, who has owned it since about 1962, was not available to get it out while I was there, so I'll have to settle for a slightly grainy photo he took of it in front of his house about ten years ago. The truck looks the same—it looks good, doesn't it?—but he doesn't get it out often these days.

Gordy Brown started doing custom paint and striping in Salt Lake, but in the mid 1960s moved his shop to the San Fernando Valley for a period. As Gordy tells it, Roth bought the black pickup with a shortened bed, dropped axle, and early Chevy hooked to a 1939 Ford trans and rear. He added the bold, white outline pinstriping and named it, then turned around and sold it within a few months. It somehow went to Salt Lake City, quickly passed through a couple more owners, then ended up with Mike Carson. The truck sat and looked right, but was pretty edgy, and Mike is a fastidious, nit-picky kind of guy. Mike knew Gordy from Salt Lake, so he called him in L.A. and sent the truck out to get it "fixed." Gordy took one look at it and decided he'd have to "blow it apart down to the bare frame and start over." Which is what he did.

If you happen to have a copy of *Hot Rods by Ed "Big Daddy" Roth* by Tony Thacker, one of the few places this truck was ever featured, you'll see dramatic before-and-after black-and-white photos of it. Other than some chroming of engine and undercarriage parts, about the only thing Mike and Gordy changed on it were the white Kelsey wires and blackwalls in place of whitewalls with baby moons. It even appears that the copious white tuck-and-roll upholstery inside was simply dyed black. You can clearly see that the body is mirror straight, the panel fit is perfect, and the Diamond Black enamel Gordy sprayed in 1963 or so looks like hand-rubbed lacquer, as it still does today. And the classic white, outline "stagecoach" striping is by Gordy, not Roth (even though it mimics the original).

When Gordy finished redoing the truck, he took it on a tour of shows up and down the West Coast, where it won first in class wherever it was shown, as it did once Mike got it back to Salt Lake City. Then, when the street rod movement got going and Joe and Lois Mayall started the Yellowstone Run, Mike drove the pickup to the first and several consecutive ones. However, as Gordy tells it, when Mike continued to show the truck locally and started getting second-place trophies "Because you've won too much," he finally relegated the good-looking little pickup to the garage, where it has spent most of the last 30-plus years. Lost.

The Ayala/Geisler GMC Pickup

Gil Ayala's first calling-card vehicle was a chopped, dark-metallic-green and brutally pale-green-flamed, 1951 GMC long-bed pickup. Not only did the truck display the Ayala's talents for custom metal work and painting (especially the filled hood, which had a row of louvers in the middle, where the seam used to be), it also boldly announced the shop's name in large chrome lettering in the middle of the grille and tailgate. This might not have added to the truck's aesthetics, but it was surely effective advertising, especially when the truck got a two-page feature in the May 1953 *Hop Up*, plus three pages in the very first *Rod & Custom* that same month.

But, despite its chrome running boards and glossy lacquer, this pickup was no showpiece; it was a hardworking shop truck. Not only did it haul parts and sit on the corner to advertise the shop but, given Gil's good nature, he'd also loan it to anyone who needed it. Joe Bailon tells how, when he drove *Miss Elegance* down for the first Motorama show, and had nothing to drive when he got there, Gil befriended him and let him use the just-chopped truck even though it had no windows.

At the same time, well-known rodder and Bonneville racer, Bruce Geisler, was growing up in the neighborhood. His father owned a large construction company near Olympic and Atlantic. Bruce saw the truck sitting on the corner every day, but said it got "run into the ground." Even though Gil repainted it a few times, including one of his candy-red jobs, Bruce said that within a few years he saw the truck sitting in the back, on four flat tires. He stopped and asked if it was for sale, and Gil said, "OK." This was sometime between 1954 and 1956.

Being a hot rodder, the first thing Bruce did was install a hot 270-ci GMC with five carburetors. But he also wanted a good-looking rig, so he added plenty of chrome, reinstalled a stock grille, and mounted chrome sidepipes along the bed. Stumped for a color, he asked his mother, who suggested a light pink from the 1956 Lincoln. Then Bruce followed Gil's example by adding the name of the family company in bold lettering on both doors. In this form the truck was featured in the March 1958 issue of *Rod & Custom*, where Editor Spence Murray claimed that it (in Gil's version) was the initial inspiration for the *Rod & Custom Dream Truck*.

Despite its show condition and overbuilt engine, Bruce drove the truck daily. But before it got run into the ground again, Bruce traded it straight across for a new 1958 Chevy at Grotewold Motors in Le Mars, Iowa. Why Iowa? If you know Bruce, you don't ask.

The truck was never seen again. That is, not until fellow zany hot rodder Dave Gorges spotted what he thought was a familiar chopped GMC pickup cab stacked on top of a pile in a wrecking yard along the highway in Albuquerque, New Mexico. This was in the early 1990s; and how it got there, nobody knows. But Dave told Bruce, Bruce went to look, and sure enough, it was his old truck. It was even in pretty good shape. So he dragged it home and rebuilt it, including the same chrome running boards, bed pipes, spotlights, lettering on the doors, and Cad wheelcovers.

This time he painted the pink in suede so he wouldn't have to worry about it, and in place of the five-carb Jimmy he substituted a 6-71 GMC-blown 383 small-block Chevy. With a stout trailer hitch on the back, he now uses it to tow his blown 1953 Stude to the dry lakes and Bonneville, and his 6-71-blown Deuce hiboy up to Washington for summer vacations. That's Bruce. The photo of the truck at El Mirage was taken in 1995. Since then he's been driving it into the ground.

Tom Pollard's 1929 A Roadster

Without question, one of the wildest magazine covers of the "little book" era has to be the June 1957 *Car Craft*, featuring George Sein's 1932 five-window in Rustic Bronze/Honduras Maroon paint covered with frantic lime-green flames, and Tom Pollard's 1929 roadster with the colors reversed and the "crab claw" flames not only licking under the 1927 T windshield, but even out of each small louver in the cycle fenders. These aren't the prettiest flames ever painted by any means, but embellished with lots of bold white-and-yellow pinstriping by both Von Dutch and Dean Jeffries, these are two of the most dynamic paint jobs ever applied to hot rods. The paint jobs were especially dynamic when the two cars were placed side by side, as they were on that cover and in a Barris booth at the 1954 Pan Pacific Motorama car show, where Dutch striped Pollard's just-painted car as spectators watched. Where are they now? Well, the Pollard car sits about 15 minutes away from my house. We all thought the Sein coupe was gone (many had searched for it in vain), but you'll see it next.

The Pollard roadster might have appeared on more magazine covers than any other I can think of. The first time was the August 1954 issue of *Rod & Custom*, when it was red with a yellow four-carb flathead. It next made the January 1955 cover of *Hot Rod*, with blond-haired Pollard pointing out details to Jack Webb of TV's *Dragnet*. But it, like the Barris crests on the cowl and the NHRA decal on the firewall, was a prop. Bart Root's similar black roadster was the "Big Rod" on the TV show, and Pollard's red one never appeared inside *Hot Rod*. But it was Barris who arranged the colorful cover, and who talked Pollard into the wild new paint job in time for the winter 1954 show and plenty more magazine covers to come.

In all this coverage it was never mentioned that this classic roadster with some unique features was actually built by Kazar "Cozy" Simonian, beginning in 1947, with some of his pals in the East L.A. Vultures car club (the same club Joe Nitti and George Bentley belonged to). Ruben Miranda boxed the 1932 rails, made the V'd spreader bar, split the wishbones, and added a stretch-drop Bell I-beam axle. Then Cozy had George Karabedian rework the 1929 body, filling the cowl, frenching the door hinges, adding flat panels in the wheelwells, and not only molding a 1940 dash to the body, but

through the 1950s, but by the 1960s Tom had had enough police chasing and sold it in 1963 to Tim Miller of San Gabriel.

Miller owned the car for a decade, and that was a time of major change for hot rods. No one seems to know much about him, but the short version is that there was an engine or electrical fire that scorched the cowl and interior. Miller replaced the flathead with a 283 Chevy mated to the 1940 trans, had the car painted in a greenish-gold with burgundy-hued flames, changed the whitewalls to blackwalls with steel rims with Ford caps, had it reupholstered in black in a style that looks very much like Joe Perez', and at some point fitted rare Kinmont disc brakes on the front. He did retain the Barris crests on the filled cowl, as well as all the car's unique styling cues such as the faired hinges, T windshield, Pontiac taillights, V'd spreader bar, split bones, and the custom 1940 dash.

Enter Richard Loe. A member of the Vintage Tin street rod club, he saw the 1929 parked at a local gas station in 1968 and says, "It was the neatest roadster I'd ever seen." When he learned it was the Pollard car, he wanted it even more. But it took until 1973 to convince Miller to sell. There's more to the story, during which the car came and went and the louvered hood sides and cycle fenders disappeared (as told in a five-page "Milestones" article in the November 2003 *Street Rodder*). But the car has been sitting in Loe's garage in La Canada now since 1977, along with several other vintage vehicles. He does clean and drive it occasionally, as he tries to decide which version to restore it to. It's tough. But this famous hot rod is well-preserved. It appeared in the 2010 Grand National Road Show "Cover Car" display.

also recessing a full set of S-W gauges in it—one of the highlights of this car. At the same time, he reworked the cowl to accept the more-svelte 1927 T cut-down windshield frame and posts, and also chopped and peaked the 1932 grille and shell to fit. After installing a two-carb Evans-equipped Flathead with chrome headers by Vultures founder Jim Deleo, Cozy had Al Ayala mix and spray a reddish-brown metallic he called "cherry coke." Finally it was trimmed in eggshell-white rolls and pleats.

This is how Pollard acquired the car, less engine, in 1953. Tom built his own very hot Flathead engine for it, and a friend's father painted it bright-red enamel. Apparently his favorite pastime with the car was street racing, at which he was quite successful, but it soon became well-known to the police around Monterey Park, where he lived. For the full story on how Tom sanded and prepped the car at Barris's for the green-and-flamed paint job, and when, where, and how Dutch striped it, I refer you to a detailed account in my book *Von Dutch: The Art, The Myth, The Legend*. The car was seen on four or five more magazines

The George Sein 1932

This may not be the most amazing story in this book, but it certainly was one of the most surprising. It's a classic "If you're looking for those kinds of cars, well there's this one here in town," scenario. I went to Pueblo, Colorado, to photograph Russell DeSalvo's black three-window Deuce. But I think it was Tom Pagano (originally from Pueblo) who told me there was "A Barris 1932 coupe from the 1950s in town that we called 'The Flamer' that's still in Ray Santistevan's garage." Santistevan was a well-known custom painter and pinstriper in the Pueblo area from the 1960s, but I had never heard of him, and I had chased an awful lot of supposed Barris cars that weren't. But the more Pagano described the car, the more it sounded like the George Sein '32. What would it be doing in Pueblo, of all places?

Then the name Zupan came up. Brothers Johnny and Joe were also (surprisingly) Pueblo natives, who ran an excavation heavy-equipment company, as well as a few Conoco gas stations in town. But they were also into customs, traveling back and forth to Los Angeles, where they were good friends and customers of the Barris brothers. Johnny had acquired the Bettancourt chopped Merc and had the Barrises update it. The Zupans also had the Barrises build a green-scalloped custom F-100 pickup. And somewhere along the line, around 1959 or 1960, Joe somehow got the lime-green-flamed Sein 1932 coupe. Also in this time period, John was killed in a tragic heavy-equipment accident. The Merc ended up at Dean Jeffries', and Joe moved back to Pueblo with the F-100 and the Sein 1932 to run his excavation business and gas stations. Locals say they saw the flamed Deuce sitting on the corner in front of one of the stations in the early 1960s.

So when I arrived in Pueblo after a long two-day drive from L.A., Jack Lee was waiting in my hotel lobby to take me to see *The Flamer*. He was pretty sure he remembered where Santistevan lived, but he hadn't been able to reach him that day. This was sounding iffy to me. But we got in Jack's truck and headed several miles out of town, drove down a small loop road, and near the end found a house with a large garage/shop out back with old cars parked around it. It was

growing dark, but Jack said this must be the place and he thought he saw somebody moving inside the lighted house.

I rang the bell, and yes, it was Santistevan, and yes, he had the Zupan/Sein coupe in the shop, and yes, we were welcome to see it and take pictures of it. Wow! A major Colorado thunderstorm was about to let loose as he opened the shop door and moved out a bright-yellow, big-block-powered 1938 Olds. Over in one corner was a candy-red, Weber-carbed early Corvette. And there was lots of other such stuff. But right in front of us was an unchopped, black-and-gray-primered 1932 coupe with a recently installed and detailed dual-quad early Cadillac engine in front of a yellow, fully pinstriped stock firewall. The front fenders were off, but the fender braces and the front crossmember were rusty chrome, as was the whole front suspension.

Ray is not a talkative guy, but as we stared at this long-lost gem of hot rod history, he started pulling parts out of shelves and rafters: the sculpted grille shell and horizontal-bar chrome grille, the nerf bars, the headlights, steering wheel, and so on. "It's all here," he said with a grin. In fact, he had heard about

the 75th anniversary of the Deuce gala (of which this was judged one of the "75 Most Significant 1932 Fords"), so he had begun to restore the car for that. But this is as far as he got. Here's the brief story:

When Zupan brought the Deuce to Pueblo, it had already sat outside and the paint was starting to check. But after a couple of harsh Colorado winters, the 40 coats of lacquer just cracked and "went to the dogs," as Ray put it. So Joe parked it in his big warehouse with his heavy equipment (along with the F-100). Joe and Santistevan were good friends (in fact, Joe got Ray to start pinstriping). So by the mid 1960s Joe brought the coupe over to Ray's with the intention of rebuilding it for his teenage son.

Workers in the warehouse had apparently accidently hit the coupe a couple of times ("They're tearing it up, Ray" was how Joe put it). One front fender was bent and the right rear quarter was "caved in." So Ray and his crew immediately stripped what flaking paint remained, repaired the damage, and primed the body. Zupan was going to put a small-block Chevy in the car for his son to drive to high school, but then thought twice and bought him a new Camaro instead. So this was 1966 or 1967. The coupe sat at Ray's shop for awhile, but then Zupan needed some of his big equipment repainted. So he told Santistevan, "You just keep the coupe and take care of this stuff for me."

It may have been a couple more years before Zupan brought over the original Cad engine, parts like the nerf bars, and a big box full of things like interior pieces and so on. Ray said he has everything for the car, including the louvered four-piece hood and even the "Kustoms L.A." plaque for the rolled-

and-louvered rear pan. But Ray said he knew little of the car's heritage. Plus it was the 1970s, and he was painting, striping, and building show cars. So by 1980, Ray had installed a 6-71-blown small-block Chevy in the coupe, along with a Corvette IRS, and painted the car a stunning, deep plum candy (the color still on the grille shell). Thankfully, he left everything on the exterior and in the interior as it was—nerfs, grille, rolled pan, bobbed fenders, etc. He said he drove the car like this for about a year, taking it to a couple local rod runs (the NSRA hadn't come to town by then). It must have been beautiful, but nobody recognized what it had been. And soon Ray was on to other more-contemporary projects, including a full schedule of painting pearls, candies, graphics, and pinstripes for customers.

It wasn't until this century, with a growing awareness of hot rod "provenance," that Ray said it was actually his wife who suggested he should probably restore the coupe to its original, lime-green-flamed and heavily pinstriped configuration. Fortunately the original Cad engine was still there, in good condition, as was the rest of the driveline (the only change Ray made was to install a rare 1937 Cad LaSalle trans in place of the original 1939 Ford box—a wise move). Much of the original black frieze and white rolled upholstery must be replaced (including the white rolled-top insert). But one of the highlights of the car today is the cracked but still wonderfully intact dashboard, not only heavily striped by Dean Jeffries and signed "56," but also adorned by a pair of monkeys hanging from it, plus another in the middle of the steering wheel.

Further, the 7-gallon Moon tank that once

mounted in the trunk has been sitting on Ray's basement desk for years, with more Jeffries striping, a gnarly finger, and an "Exhibit of Honour" plaque from the 1956 Oakland Roadster Show. Ray says he has already matched a couple of gallons of paint to samples of the Rustic Bronze Metallic he found on the car, and mixing up the lime gold is no problem. Nor is laying out the frenetic flames or adding the copious white-and-yellow pinstriping—that's what Ray has been doing for decades. Now it's just a matter of getting it done. It's all there. He's got a good start. What a find!

The Chuck Porter Pickup

Most of the research for this book has been fun, but some has been frustrating. Most of us know the Chuck Porter chopped, channeled, sectioned, and shortened '40 Ford pickup from its cover and four-page story in the March 1955 issue of *Hot Rod*. He had just finished painting it 1955 T-Bird Goldenrod Yellow. The fact that Porter's custom body shop was just a few blocks from *Hot Rod's* offices at 5959 Hollywood Boulevard facilitated taking pictures of this amazing truck's construction from the frame up, much of which was shown in the article, including the extensive body surgery. Chuck was an inveterate racer as well as a highly talented metal man. Many fail to realize that he incorporated both passions in this pickup.

At first it looks like a low, slinky, streamlined "lead sled." But there was no lead in this truck. Chuck may have reduced all of its dimensions to make it look better, but really it was to make it much lighter, for acceleration. The original frame is not only severely cut down, but also drilled full of large lightening holes. He even went so far as to replace the truck dual-leaf front I-beam with a 1939 Ford tube axle, single cross-spring, and 1934 steering box to lower and lighten the truck. The abbreviated bed is completely

made of sheet aluminum. Then he fit it with a big, brawny (yet impeccably detailed) Max Balchowski-built, bored-and-stroked 1953 Cadillac engine, which he set back in the frame as far as possible for improved traction. This truck was both a looker and a sleeper that won its share on strip and street.

I first saw the truck at one of the last Renegades car shows in Long Beach in the early 1970s, but it was parked in a hallway. It had the Cad engine, but I can't remember if it was still yellow or already had some flames painted on it. I thought someone other than Chuck owned it, but that's fuzzy. I also first met

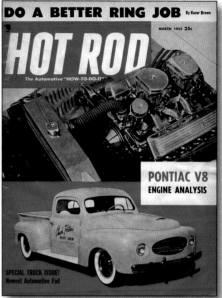

Chuck briefly about this time at his shop in Hollywood. I remember there were sports- and sprint-type race cars in the shop and Duffy Livingstone's race-T was sitting in a corner (another amazing "lost rod" story I was involved in, that has been told in a full book by current owner Brock Yates).

The next time I saw this truck was in the late 1980s or early 1990s, either at a Road Kings car show in Burbank, as shown in my black-and-white photo, or at Paso Robles, as seen on page 56 in Andy Southard's book *Hot Rods of the 1950s*. At this point someone had radiused and flared the fenders for wide-oval tires on chrome rims, removed the aluminum running boards, and painted it red with blue/yellow/orange flames. However, the dual-quad Cad engine appears to still be in the truck, as well as the beautiful brass radiator.

Chuck died in 1982, at speed at the wheel of one of his restored Kurtis Offy midgets. Debby Porter, his daughter, who now has acquired the truck, claims that 14 people owned it in between, including four in Oklahoma. What I know is that in the last 8 to 10 years I saw this truck, painted a single metallic maroon with a louvered tailgate and billet wheels, bombing around the Glendale-Burbank area on several occasions. It looked well-used (not well-kept). For some reason I thought it had a Ford engine in it. I met the owner one time, and his attitude was "This is my truck and I'll do what I want with it." Well...

Recently I learned that Debby Porter had the truck. She told me that she had put an ad in *Hemmings*, with a photo, asking "Have you seen this truck?" with no results. Then she made up a small, similar sign and put it in her windshield while parked at the Bob's Cruise Night in Toluca Lake. Bingo! Since the truck was in the area, someone knew the owner and put Debby in touch. She said the truck had been sitting in his garage for 14 years, and he didn't want to sell.

She didn't explain how she convinced him, but she got the truck back a couple years ago. It suffered a subsequent brake failure and crunched the right front corner, which led to installing a new tube front axle on air bags with disc brakes. Next she took it to Mike Fennel's huge custom/restoration shop in Saugus to get the damage repaired, the wheelwells returned to original shape, and a new tailgate and running boards made, in preparation for a repaint to the Goldenrod Yellow. Good.

So yesterday I jumped in my car and drove up there to get the latest photos you see here. The body is now very close to original, the aluminum bed is perfect, the dash is still full of early S-W gauges, and it has proper wheels and tires on it. My biggest surprise was to see that it still has a dual-quad Cadillac engine in the original location. Apparently it's a later model, the manifold/carbs and valve covers have been changed, and somebody went nuts plating everything copper (and of course it has some sort of late auto trans in it). The whole truck is surprisingly intact, original, and now awaiting repainting. For much more info on Chuck and the truck, hopefully with updates, visit Debby's website on him: www.Chuck-Porter.com. For a look at Debby's own multi-faceted career as a movie/TV stuntwoman, country singer, and current caretaker of endangered crows and ravens, go to www.DebbyPorter.com.

The Woods/Block/Unger T

When I mentioned to Dan Woods not long ago that one of the guys in my car club had one of his Ts that was originally built for well-known street rod and show-car owner Bill Block of Wisconsin, Dan unhesitatingly replied, "That's the nicest T I ever built." That's saying a whole lot, because Dan Woods built *many* of the nicest T-buckets and show rods ever built. I don't think anyone who knows hot rods would argue that, whether you happen to care for the tall-top, brass lights, and wire wheel style of his 1970s-era cars or not.

But let's start this story with Brent Unger, who lives near the Rose Bowl in Pasadena (where I took these photos in the parking lot). Like so many of his generation, he fell for Kookie's car on *77 Sunset Strip* on TV. In the latter 1960s Brent and his brother Milt (both now active members of the Street Rods Forever club) actually started gathering components to build a T-bucket. They had a body, a frame, and an engine. But Brent was called to Vietnam, the project stalled,

and the parts were sold off. That was as close as Brent came to building or owning any hot rod, let alone a *Kookie T*.

Then (and isn't this how these stories go—meaning any which way?), in 1998 Brent was driving to Lake Tahoe on a business trip, and stopped in Fresno for the night. Having nothing better to do, after dinner he went out for a cruise down the main drag. Somewhere along the route he passed a big glass storefront that had several cars inside for sale. The one in front, next to the window, was a wild, tall-top, bright-orange *Kookie T*. Brent jammed on the brakes and hung a U-turn for a better look. The place was a specialty cars consignment dealer, which of course was closed, but Brent jotted down the phone number that was on the door. The next day he called from Tahoe, and made arrangements to meet the car's owner, Jess Pendercraft, on his way back home.

At that time, Brent admits, he didn't know who Dan Woods was, he didn't know the significance of a

accident upon its return from the interior shop." But there is no further explanation.

Brent figures he's the third owner of the T, but has no idea who painted the orange-pearl lacquer, added the gold-leaf striping, did the unexplainable mural on the gas tank, or redid the dark brown velvet upholstery and the top with the "tea cup" rear window. He said it had blue/yellow "T Cup" plates on it when he got it (different from the ones in the Block photos). But almost everything on the car remains as he bought it in 1998: a Jim Babb brass radiator, Steve Davis aluminum oval gas tank, Jag rear with Woods' machined hub carriers, and 289 Ford engine fitted with rare Gurney-Weslake Indy-car heads.

Gurney-Weslake engine, and Pendercraft "Didn't go into much detail." The main thing Brent ascertained was that the car ran and operated properly. They agreed on a price, and Brent bought it on the spot. Later, as Brent learned more about his T, he contacted legendary Fresno show promoter Blackie Gejeian, who of course knew of the car and knew Pendercraft (whom he said had since passed away), but didn't have much further information.

The car has a few chips and battle scars, and from that Brent guessed that it was originally brown. In fact, a recent issue of *The Rodder's Journal* (No. 43), with an article on Dan Woods' career, shows two photos of what appears to be this car (owned by Bill Block), in a medium-brown paint job with tan vinyl upholstery and a tan top (with a rectangular window), and with brass cowl lamps and horn. The single caption ends: "The tall T-top was crushed in a bizarre

About the only changes he has made are adding Wilwood brake calipers (front and rear) with newer tires for streetability, tuning the carbs, plus reworking the headlight stands to keep them from breaking off. Otherwise Brent has simply been preserving this wonderful piece of hot rod history and driving the wheels off it. He generally takes it out once or twice a week, year-round.

After our photo session, with me riding shotgun, he took a decidedly long way home. I've ridden in a lot of T-buckets, Weber-carbureted rods, and even other Woods-built machines with opposed-coil front ends that neither rode, steered, accelerated, nor stopped as excellently as this car does. With its well-tuned Jag rear, extended front axle, and very light weight, this T handled potholed straightaways and twisty mountain roads like an agile sports car. All T-buckets should ride so well and be driven as often.

The Glen Hooker 1939 Mercury

Neil Emory and Clayton Jensen's Valley Custom is regarded—certainly by me—as one of the best of all the 1940s, 1950s, and 1960s custom shops, for quality of work and clean design. However, perhaps because of the high quality of their work, it lacked in quantity. You can count the famous Valley Customs on little more than two hands. I knew where most of them were and kept tabs on them for years, such as the *Polynesian* in Gene Blackford's Red Lacquer Room in Ohio and the Dick Flint roadster in Duane Kofoed's garage (both now restored), plus the Ray Vega 1938 convertible sedan, which is very slowly being restored. The Ralph Jilek black, sectioned 1940 Ford, beautifully finished for Pebble Beach by Tom Gloy, recently sold at the Whitworth auction, and is now gone to an unknown new home.

But the Glen Hooker 1939 Mercury convertible, sometimes confused with the Jilek car, was the one that was missing. In a recent two-part story on Valley Custom, Spence Murray noted that stories about this car tended to be embellished or misstated, concluding, "Its whereabouts today are unknown."

That's a bit surprising, since Spence was in contact with family members who even supplied him with the two excellent photos of this car shown here, probably taken in the Hooker front yard around 1955. The rare color photo shows what I think was Titian Red (or Tahitian, a 1953 Buick color) with a long black scallop outlined in white (other photos show a smaller scallop just on the door, above the chrome strip). In these photos, with the white Carson top removed, a tarp covers the rear seat.

Starting at the beginning, Neil and Clay Jensen married to two sisters, named Hooker, and their younger brother was Glen, not yet in high school. As he neared driving age, his grandfather presented Glen with a 1939 Mercury convertible (or most of one), and employed Neil and Clay to "fix it up" for him. So, rather than commissioned by a well-to-do paying customer, from the beginning this was sort of a low-buck family project. I assume that may be why a 1940 front end was used (the original being wrecked?). It is certainly why the body was not sectioned (as on the Jilek car), but rather channeled over the frame, with the running boards removed and the fenders trimmed at

Washington state. Glen called Gordy in Salt Lake; Gordy said, "Let's go get it," so they did, taking it up to Washington with Gordy's truck and trailer.

By this time the Carson top was a bare frame, and there was a 1950s Cadillac engine inside the car, on a pallet, though the original driveline was still in place. Gordy stayed a week to help Glen strip the car to very good, non-rusted bare metal, and spray it with black primer/sealer. In the following years Glen decided to install the early Cad engine in the car, along with a Mustang II front suspension, air bags, and other upgrades. Also, after consulting with Neil and being encouraged by him to do so, Glen decided to section the hood about 1½ inches, dropping the cowl/lower windshield to match. Glen did all of this work at home, with the help of a good welder friend. And you must remember it was *his* car.

the bottoms and the wheel openings cut higher. According to Gordy Brown, the car's current owner, they even found a "used" Carson top to fit the body, and then cut the windshield to match it.

Also according to Brown, the car was finished even before Glen got his license. He drove it through high school and a few years after. Then he sold it to someone in L.A., either right before or after it was featured in a B movie titled *A Strange Adventure*. Glen went on to pursue various careers, continuing to own and build other cars. The Merc got painted refrigerator white at some point, then ended up abandoned, intact but weathered, in a California desert wrecking yard.

Then, sometime in the 1980s, a vintage-car buyer/seller from the East Coast and/or Arizona found the car, figured what it might be, and located Glen (who was then taking Neil to custom car events, such as Paso Robles) to verify it. Once verified, the seller advertised the car in *Hemmings* for big dollars, but there were no takers.

To shorten the story quite a bit, Gordy Brown, a long-time custom car builder and painter from Salt Lake City, was friends with Neil and Glen. I'm leaving a lot out, but the seller finally called Glen, offering him the car for a price that was high, but affordable. It was in Arizona, and Glen was then in

This is where the story turns a bit noir. We can't go into it, but in the late 1990s Glen had to leave Washington, so he offered the car, as it was, to Gordy, who offered to buy it and keep it. And that's what he's been doing since. It sits, as you see it, in Gordy's large warehouse in Salt Lake City, a bit updated, but in excellent and very complete condition.

El Capitola

If you want to find a rare, lost, famous old custom, don't try this. It doesn't work very often. In fact, it's called serendipity, which is something you have no control over, whatsoever.

El Capitola was the last custom built by Sam Barris. Sam left Barris Kustom City in Lynwood sometime before the shop fire of December 1957 and returned to Sacramento. Although he was working as an insurance adjuster, he was doing some custom work on the side, out of his garage.

He did considerably more than "some" work on *El Capitola* (obviously named after the city, capital of California), which started as a near-new 1957 Chevy 210 coupe. Sam chopped it, made it a hardtop, added 1957 Lincoln fins, and so many other changes it's very difficult to identify the car. Then he sent it down to have George (or possibly Junior at that point) paint it fuschia candy over white pearl, as seen in the original front-end photo. Then Eddie Martinez did the upholstery, including swivel bucket seats and a TV in the

back, in gold frieze and white tuck-and-roll. The car was built for Don Fletcher, who later sold it to Virgil Brinkman. I have no idea how it got to Ohio, or who painted the red part gold.

Enter Guy Boucher of Lewiston, Maine, a longtime hot rodder, drag racer, and customizer who had a couple of 1932 Ford roadsters in high school, raced a Top Fuel car in the 1970s, and about ten years ago built a chopped 1949 Merc in the same colors and similar appearance as the Hirohata '51. Having finished the Merc, Guy decided it was time to build another 1932, and called Brookville Roadster, in Brookville, Ohio, to order one of its new steel bodies. In discussing this with owner Ray Gollahon, Guy mentioned he had just built a full custom. "Oh, we have one of those," Ray replied. "It's an early Barris car." I'm always skeptical when someone says something like that, especially in the middle of Ohio, but this got Guy's attention. When Ray told him which car it was, he got real interested.

Dig this story: The car actually belonged to Ray and his brother Chuck's 92-year-old mother, Eula. She bought it nearly 40 years prior for Chuck's son. Why she did this has not been explained, because Ray's son, Kenny, is very much into cars and the family business building steel bodies for early Fords, but Chuck's son is into karate, to the point that he has made several films with Chuck Norris. He had no interest in the car, so it sat in grandma Eula's garage for 40 years.

It took Guy nearly a year to talk Eula out of the car. But when he finally did and trailered it (and a new steel Deuce roadster body) home to Maine, it looked just as you see it in the other photo when he rolled it into his driveway: totally rust-free; complete down to the spotlights, Barris crests, and even the rare cast-aluminum wheelcovers; and running with only 30,000 miles on the odometer. The Eddie Martinez upholstery was excellent, and the chrome was even in good shape. Mrs. Gollahon must have had a very dry, tight garage, because most cars, especially big customs like this with lots of lavish upholstery, suffer seri-

ous mildew and rust in the Midwest and East when stored that long. In the photo, taken in 1999, not only is the white pearl neither yellowed nor faded, but even the whitewall tires look like new!

Guy said the only thing the car really needed was a rebuild of the mechanicals, and a repaint, since not only had the color been changed, but the 40 coats of 40-year-old lacquer were beginning to check. So Guy rebuilt the engine (which turned out to be a "leftover" 265 in this early-production 1957) and brakes, leaving the stock column-shift 3-speed in place, and spent a year carefully scraping all the paint off the car with razor blades, so as not to harm any of the original (and perfect) Sam Barris lead work. He then repainted it in the correct candy fuschia over white pearl, using modern basecoat/clearcoat.

Since then, Guy has moved on to his next project, restoring Tommy Ivo's last front-engine dragster (which is done and running) and one of his Funny Cars. But he says *El Capitola* is one of his "keepers." It sits in the garage and gets driven around town whenever he feels like it—as it should.

The Phil Kendrick *Super Prune* 1932 Sedan

This chopped 1932 sedan has led a long, varied, and somewhat tumultuous life. It was first seen in a close-up photo on the cover of the April 1958 issue of *Car Craft*, featuring its yellow-painted 3-71-blown flathead engine, along with then-owner Dave Archer. You can barely see it has a chopped top with a white roof insert and white upholstery; the car is red with a black firewall, and it has King Bee headlights and a filled grille shell. However, the cover touts a story on blowers, and the car is neither seen inside, nor in any other magazines I could find.

It gained fame when it appeared as a two-page color feature in the April 1967 issue of *Hot Rod*, simply titled "Flawless!" The car was then owned by Phil Kendrick of Oakland, California, who had replaced the rear of the body, which had been smashed. The paint was then bright orange by Tony Del Rio, with characteristic, subtle black-and-white striping by Tommy the Greek. Kendrick removed the stock gas tank and frame horns, and bobbed the rear fenders (adding six small louvers to each), to show off a fully polished and chromed quick-change rear end on a Model A spring, with handmade polished-and-drilled aluminum nerf bars. Big and little Firestone Blue Streak racing tires were mounted on similar-sized polished Halibrand magnesium wheels. Strangely, a single truck-type taillight was mounted on the left side. A three-carb 265 Chevy engine sat in front of a smooth, chromed firewall.

In keeping with the times, the interior was redone in all-black tuck-and-roll, including light, swivel bucket seats. With the chopped top, orange paint, and pronounced rake, it was a striking, racy image. At the same time nearly everything under the car was chromed and impeccably detailed. It won the Sweepstakes award at its first show, and racked up many more trophies, including repeated showings at Oakland. Because of this, Kendrick was asked to "redo" the car, and he sort of retaliated by painting it a pale pearl yellow, with wispy green/orange pearl flames, and the name "Super Prune" lettered boldly across the back, with a purpley blob (prune?) below it that actually was a tangle of naked women (if you looked closely).

Then it disappeared for about ten years until guitarist and hot rod enthusiast/builder Jeff Beck heard it was available (through Roy Brizio), bought it, and shipped it to England, where you see it sitting in his "carriage house" next to his duplicate of the *American Graffiti* coupe that he built himself. After a few years, with the chrome beginning to rust, Jeff realized the car wasn't suited to the damp English climate, and sold it (again through Brizio) to the DeMarco brothers, Frankie and Joey, in the mid 1980s. Substituting the chrome engine and early Ford driveline with standard 350/9-inch/4-bar components, Joey used it to deliver products for Frankie's Rosemead, California, automotive paint store, and as a typical street beater, until it again got crunched in the rear.

This car was rightfully (in my strong opinion) voted one of the "75 Most Significant 1932 Ford Hot Rods," as presented by Ford at the 2007 Grand National Roadster Show in Pomona. For that event, the DeMarcos were able to get the rear of the body repaired and the original quick-change/driveline reinstalled, though the car was shown in bare metal and gray primer. In the most recent photo shown here, it was in Derek Bower's shop getting the original front axle and drilled split wishbones replaced. The chrome firewall is there, the engine has three carbs, and the front nerfs are in place. However, the orange paint was a quickie test/preservative coat, and what you can't see is a pair of rear frame horns and a stock gas tank being installed (the original one in the back seat area was too much hassle). That was about a year ago, and the car hasn't been seen since, so I have no idea what its future will be.

Morawski's Cars

rank Morawski owns a small business in Bel Air, Maryland, called The Glass Shop, which makes fiberglass parts for 1953 Studebakers and does custom fiberglass work, mostly for race cars. I would not call him a car collector, but rather an opportunist. He has three significant vehicles, and he got each of them when the opportunity presented itself.

How did he get the famous *Super Bell* coupe? Simple, he bought it in the 1980s from Jim Ewing, the car's builder and founder of the Super Bell Axle Company, when Jim decided he'd done just about everything he wanted to do with it. Previously fitted with big- and small-block Chevy V-8s, it currently has a cross-country Buick V-6 and unpolished Halibrand wheel combination. I wouldn't call this hot rod lost, necessarily, but you might not have known it's been living, and continues driving, on the East Coast.

Next is the Fred Carrillo rear-engine 1927 T lakes roadster that was featured on the cover of the July 1953 *Hot Rod* magazine when it was yellow, along with a full Rex Burnett cutaway in the four-page layout inside. Frank saw this car advertised in *Hemmings* as an "old Indy-area race car" in the late 1970s. The owner didn't know what it was, the price was right, and Frank took a chance. He later contacted Carrillo himself, who identified parts of the car to verify it was his. Frank has been collecting parts and piecing this one back together slowly. The photo shows it mocked up in primer, engineless, at a recent Baltimore vintage rod show.

But the car that led me to contact Frank is his more recent acquisition, the far-less-famous Curley Tremayne chopped 1950 Merc from Salinas, California. This car is significant to me because when I did the Special Chopped Merc issue of *Street Rodder* magazine in August 1977, when I was pushing for a custom car revival, this was one of only a dozen chopped 1949–1951 Mercs we could find in the country to feature! Besides that, I still think it's one of the best proportioned, with its smooth rear roof, slightly slanted B-pillars, nicely rounded hood corners, and thematic frenched 1954 Buick headlights and 1950 taillights. The grille bar is the only non-traditional part, which comes from a 1964 Buick Wildcat. Plus candy

Curley drove the car regularly on the street for years, finally spraying red primer in areas where the candy lacquer inevitably began to check. Unfortunately Curley's health also began to fail, and he passed away in 1998, leaving the car's fate somewhat in limbo. Frank said he was able to acquire it through Gary Minor's efforts, and he is officially the car's second owner (Curley's family bought it new). Since getting it in 2000, Frank has rebuilt the Ford Y-Block engine and all the mechanicals, but has left everything else just as he got it, including the pearl white tuck-and-roll interior, which is in very good condition. So this one isn't lost; it's saved.

tangerine is one of my favorite colors, and this excellent example was sprayed by my friend Rod Powell. Curley worked in Rod's Salinas, California, custom shop at the time and helped metal man Butch Hurlhey do the roof and other modifications.

The Jimmy Summers Merc

First, if the pictures on page 111 look a little fuzzy, that's because they are "spy" photos. Second, I probably wouldn't believe this story if I hadn't written it myself, and even then I'm not sure how much is true. This car is legendary, and you know how legends go.

Jimmy Summers, who opened his Hollywood shop in the 1930s, was a pioneer customizer (and reputedly one of the best, ever), but little is known of him because he predated custom car magazines. This might be the only Jimmy Summers custom to still exist, his own sectioned-and-channeled 1939 Mercury convertible, and it's incredible how intact and complete it is, especially after hearing the story. I heard most of it from Doane Spencer.

Doane and Jimmy were best friends, and for several years in the 1940s they set off on cross-country trips, either in Doane's 1932 roadster or Jimmy's 1939 convertible, stopping at Ford dealers to earn money doing mechanical or body work. The point is this Merc got driven a lot.

When Jimmy built it, he painted it GM Ruby Maroon and Carson made an unusual tan top to go with it. Sometime in the later 1940s, a Jane Mansfield–looking (and tempered) second wife entered the picture and either she drove the Merc up the courthouse steps in L.A. (or Sacramento), or Jimmy did, because...well, the car got banged up and consequently repainted the green you see in the early photo.

Then, in the early 1950s, an Air Force colonel from Texas named, of course, Tex Roberts (who's a whole other story including Indy, engines, etc.), bought the car and had Jimmy french the headlights and fill the hood top (as seen in the spy photos). Then he was sent to several locations in South America, and he took the Merc everywhere he went, which included carrying it on poles through the jungle at one point. So the story goes.

Somehow Tex and the Merc ended up in the Tacoma, Washington, area by the mid 1960s. It was in white primer and sitting outside when local rodder/customizer Dick Page saw it, somehow got it, and literally built a building around it. But then Tex got the car back, some more modifications were made, and then Dick got it back again. There are further stories of chasing the car on trailers, other cars being traded back-and-forth for it, and so on, but you get the picture.

Page says he's had the car ten years at this point, and that it's all there, with no rust. The original grille just needs replating; there's a full dash with instruments, and even the Carson top frame is complete with aviary wire. Dick says he'll un-french the headlights and license in the deck, and eventually refinish it in Ruby Maroon. But for now he's keeping this historic custom safe.

The Full-Circle T

I'm not making any of this up, I swear. In this case, I have to remember the best I can. It's the early 1970s. I'm a cub reporter just starting out with *Street Rodder* magazine. It's a Sunday afternoon, and my young wife and I are in our small apartment on the south side of Santa Ana. Suddenly I hear the roar of a huge engine and the shriek of burning rubber. I yell to Anna as I'm running out the door, "I don't know what that is, but it's got a big blower on it and it's doing a burnout down Flower Street!" I followed the sound around a couple of corners until it stopped. When I got there I saw what looked more like a Top Fuel dragster than a street roadster: a giant, rare Boss 429 Ford Hemi engine topped with a 6-71 blower; dragster-size slicks on polished mag wheels; brilliant red Metalflake body with psychedelic candy graphics; and chrome everything. The now-quiet car had wisps of oil smoke curling from the valve-cover breathers, the chrome headers were crackling from the heat, and Lou Hislop was sitting in the button-tufted seat with a large grin spread beneath his bushy mustache.

This was my first introduction to Lou and what I'll call the Urich T. Lou, who lived in Santa Ana, and who had built this fabulous car, had come to visit a rodding friend. I immediately took out a pen and notepad to get his name and number and to set up a photo shoot for the magazine. You just didn't see stuff like this on the street back then. It was the age of Fad Ts, yes. But there were no Fad Ts like this one.

It turned out the guys at the magazine knew Lou well. They had featured his much more subtle, but equally impressive black,

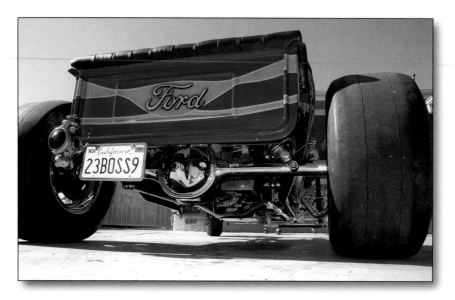

brakes, front and rear, from CAE in San Diego, with real Halibrand mag wheels to match.

But that wasn't enough. He wanted everything on this chassis, including the frame, chromed. So he went to his friend Charlie Cox, who was the foreman at Orange Coast Plating (also in Santa Ana) to do the work. Charlie had to find a bigger tank to dip the frame, but he got everything done.

A painter who simply went by "Molly" was the Art Himsl of SoCal at the time, so they gave him the fiberglass body and said, "Paint it." No further instructions. What you see is what they got. Jim Babb built the narrow brass radiator to fit. Then Bob Fehd added the contemporary button tuft in black leather. Meanwhile the blown Boss had dyno'd at 1,000+hp at Unser's, so he detuned it to 750 for young Jack, Jr., to drive!

It was all done in time to enter the major L.A. car show of the time, the Winternationals at the Great Western Exhibit Center in 1970, where it copped the Grand Sweepstakes award. Urich was pleased. The bill for the car, besides Lou's $1,000, had come to $27,000, including $10,000 for Unser alone; plus Molly, the chrome, etc. But Urich not only gave Lou a bonus, he also gave him the diamond ring that went with the Grand Sweepstakes trophy and a job with UOC. The car was featured on the cover of *Popular Hot Rodding* for March 1971, in a single color photo in Petersen's *Street Rod Pictorial* No. 3, and on a two-page black-and-white spread in *Hot Rod Yearbook* No. 10 (both in 1971) before the *Street Rodder* cover and centerspread in 1974.

Of course there's way more to this story, a small part of which I told in an early editorial column in that June 1974 *Street Rodder* magazine. Briefly: When Jr. finally turned 16 and got the car, he promptly bent the frame doing wheelstands (requiring rebracing and rechroming), got it stuck in the sand at the beach, and basically scared the pee out of himself with it. So Lou took the engine out of the T and put it in a ski boat for him. In fact, it pulled the stringers out of two boats before Jr. finally put it on a stand and forgot about it.

Jack, Sr., sold the T, less engine, to Hislop for next to nothing. Lou put a stock 429 out of a 1972 Ranchero in it and painted the body black, before trading it for a four-wheel-drive Chevy pickup in 1976 or 1977. From there it went through several owners, one of whom painted the car a light yellow and put a phony 8-71 blower and Hilborn injector on top of the single 4-barrel on the 429. I saw the car in this version

wire-wheeled, 1917 center door T street rod a couple years before. So I not only arranged to photograph the roadster, but to feature it prominently on the June 1974 cover. I was relegated to arranging the shoot, cleaning the car, and taking detail photos while Jim Clark took the cover picture from the roof of his van with a 4x5 camera.

Let me back up.... Jack Urich's family owned the Lincoln-Mercury dealership in Whittier, California, and he had started Urich Oil Company (UOC), which had gas stations throughout the local area. Somehow Jack and Lou got hooked up. Jack wanted to build a wild, show-winning T roadster—ostensibly for his son, Jack, Jr., who was 13 at the time (but also to promote the company)—so he contracted with Lou to build the car. I'm shortening the story considerably, but Lou told Jack he had a "dream car" T in his head that he wanted to build, and told Jack he'd do it for $1,000 plus the cost of building the car. Lou made some sketches and the deal was struck.

Being a Mercury dealer, Urich wanted Ford power. He had seen Connie Kalitta's Boss Hemi dragster, and decided that's what he wanted. The only other blown Ford Hemi at the time was in a Mickey Thompson Funny Car. So Urich ordered the Boss 429 in a crate from Ford. Lou got a blower manifold (and aluminum rods) from Mickey, a blower and drive from Don Hampton, and arranged for no less than Louie Unser to build and dyno this beast in his Santa Ana shop.

Meanwhile, Lou knew dragster pilot Zane Schubert, who had a chassis and machine shop in his backyard, and had another friend who worked at Dan Gurney's Indy-car shop in Santa Ana. With Schubert's help, and use of his heliarc welder, Lou laid out a double-rail, round-tube frame for the T. He got a set of then-rarely-used coil-over Koni race shocks from the friend at Gurney's to suspend it, and then ordered pin-drive sprint-car knock-off hubs, with Airheart disc

for a few years at the L.A. Roadsters' Fathers' Day show, and put a picture of it on the cover of my book, *Ford Performance,* when it was revised in 1997 (there's also a picture of the black Hislop stock 429 version inside on pg. 14). Further, some new owner called me at the *Rod & Custom* offices sometime in the mid 1990s wanting to know how to duplicate the original paint, but that apparently didn't happen then.

Somehow the car ended up in the small town of Fellows, California, west of Bakersfield, and sat outside because the owner was too old to drive it. That's the story. A guy known only as "Mike" from Yorba Linda, California, found it there around 2005 or so. He bought it, began researching its history, and ultimately restored it by sanding the body down to the original paint, making tracings of it, and having it duplicated. He also had the black leather upholstery redone, made the chrome zoomie headers, and a few other things, but kept the original chrome chassis as-is and the 429 engine with the fake blower. In this form Mike put the car on eBay in 2007 hoping to get $40,000+ for it. Unfortunately, bidding didn't reach his reserve of $15,000.

Remember Charlie Cox of the chrome shop? He has a son, Greg, who remembers sitting on a crate and hand-sanding that frame with emery cloth as part of the polishing process when he was 11 years old. He remembers riding with Lou in the finished car, a couple years later, and seeing those slicks "grow" and smoke every time he twitched the throttle.

About that time Charlie acquired Artistic Silver Plating in Signal Hill, California, and soon offered high-end chroming as well. Several years ago Greg took over the plating business, but he and his dad have remained good friends with Lou. Pay attention, because it gets complicated here.

Greg has been building cars in his garage/shop for some time, preferring Ford products with big-

block engines. He was working on an F-100 and a 1960s Mustang. Lou had kept in touch with Jack Urich, Jr., who had moved to an avocado ranch in Fallbrook. He not only had the complete blown Boss 429 out of the T ("freshened up" by Unser in 1980), but also a complete, rare, Tunnel Port 427 as well, on stands. In 2003, Jr. needed cash, put both engines up for sale, and Lou told Greg. In short, Greg bought both for a good price, put the Tunnel Port in his Mustang, and kept the blown Boss on the stand for the time being.

Meanwhile, Mike got the T and started researching it. He located Hislop in Corona, who told him Greg had the engine, plus he could do chrome work for him. There's more to it, but that's how Greg learned Mike had the car—the one he helped his dad chrome the frame on; the one he rode in with Lou as a young teen; and the one he now had the engine for. So when Greg saw the roadster up for auction on eBay in 2007, and not selling, he contacted Mike and made him an offer close to his reserve. Given the economy at the time, and the obvious unpopularity of T-buckets, Mike took it.

Greg was busy building the Mustang at the time, so he took the phony blower off the 429 and otherwise left the T as it was. But you can imagine my amazement when I saw the T, sitting next to the beautiful Tunnel Port Mustang, in a booth at the L.A. Roadsters' show in 2009. When Greg told me he had the original engine for it, too, my jaw dropped farther. I immediately made arrangements to photograph the car and engine in Greg's front yard (sort of like the 1974 *Street Rodder* cover). And then, as a total surprise to me, Greg got Lou Hislop—I hadn't seen him in 30 years—to stop by, since he was working on a job in the area that day. Wow.

That's Greg and Lou standing behind the car in the photo. So the story comes full circle. It's long and complicated, but it's a good one.

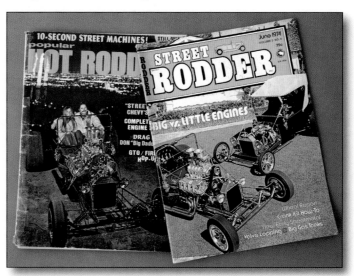

Hidden Treasure,

I could write a complete manual on "How to Seek and Find Lost Hot Rods and Treasured Famous Customs," and you could study it assiduously and follow every procedure outlined in it, and still possibly come up with nothing better than a stock 1938 Plymouth or Model-A four-door with rusted-out floors.

On the other hand, if you're the type of rodder who knows a good find when you see it, scans the "for sale" columns in periodicals and on the Internet, or are just plain lucky, every once in a while a true gem suddenly, surprisingly, appears in the trash pile or dung heap. How about the "Old Coupe" for sale that really turns out to be a 1932 three-window? Yes.

Or you see a cool rod or custom in a 1950s magazine, wonder facetiously if the same guy might still have it, call Information for his name in the town listed, and he actually answers and says, "Yes, it's right here in my garage." That sounds like a script for a Disney movie, but I have an example right here.

Or you go shopping for your first car at age 16, pick out something cheap but cool because it's customized, and later find out it was on the cover of magazines decades ago. Or, even more amazing, it turns out to be a star of an all-time blockbuster movie. Yes, it's quite rare, but I have examples of that, too. Read on.

Lucky Finds

Chapter Six

The Lien Sale Merc

Young Greg Beck of Redlands, California, is always on the lookout for cool, older, affordable cars, with the emphasis on affordable. There's a clean six-cylinder 1956 Chevy in the backyard and a four-door 1951 Merc in the driveway. The one I drove 90 miles east of L.A. to see is the mild custom 1951 with the now-crinkly Dodge Royal Blue lacquer shown here. Before I tell you what it is, let me tell you how he got it.

Greg likes to surf the internet looking for custom stuff, from old magazines to complete cars. He happened to see this Merc on eBay. It was in a storage yard in San Diego, the owner had apparently died, and the yard was doing a lien sale on the car because the relatives didn't want to pay the back rent. A big selling point, according to the listing, was a dual-quad Chrysler Hemi engine. Greg was more interested in the custom features like the frenched headlights and the 1955 DeSoto grille. So he bid on the car. However, the reserve was $10,000, which apparently nobody came close to matching. Guess what? The seller contacted Greg asking, "How much is your offer?" Greg named a number substantially less than the reserve, and the yard owner said, "OK." So Greg went down and got it.

Along with the car came a bag of receipts going back to 1959, which was when the last owner had bought it. He put a new flathead in it in 1960, then sometime in the next nine years bought and partially installed a complete 1955 Chrysler 300-C Hemi and trans (which, to the right Mopar collector, is probably worth more than what Greg paid for the whole car). Given the car's unlowered stance and the Traction Masters visible under the rear, it was being converted more for drag racing than custom cruising. But that's as far as it got. The installation was never completed. The car was last registered in 1969, and that's when it went into the storage lot. So what Greg got was fortunately frozen in time. But there were no clues to its former history.

Looking at the car today, however, it's obvious it was a show-worthy mild custom of the early 1950s. First clues are the all-chromed window frames inside, the period pinstriped dash, the real Appleton spotlights, and—one of the best things on the car—a very weathered Barris Kustoms water decal in the windshield corner. The highlight, however, is the aging blue-and-white, diamond-motif, full tuck-and-roll interior. If this wasn't done in Tijuana in the early 1950s, it was done by someone in a small shop who learned in Tijuana. With some work, it might be saved; if not, it can certainly be duplicated.

Of course there were hundreds of mild customs like this in the 1950s. But Greg posted some pictures of this one on the H.A.M.B. forum to see if anybody

recognized it, and he got lucky. Somebody remembered seeing it in a magazine. It was the July 1957 *Car Craft*, to be exact, where it appeared on one page of a 10-page feature titled "Those Marvelous Mercs" that began with Sonny Morris' and ended with Buddy Alcorn's. This one is listed as Philip Sauers'. It is shown sitting 8 inches lower with wide whites and Olds Fiesta flippers, a full-dressed flathead, and handmade round bullet taillights in the rear bumper guards.

The magazine neither says where Sauers was from, nor what color the car was (I assume the blue that's still on it). The photos were by Petersen staffer Bob D'Olivo, so I might further assume the car was from the L.A. area and ended up in San Diego by 1959, but who knows? The point is that it has been saved, it is appreciated by its new owner, and is to be restored as closely to its 1957 magazine version as Greg can manage.

The Doctor's Rod

Kurt McCormick is unquestionably the premiere restorer and collector of early Barris and related customs, including the *Rod & Custom Dream Truck*, the Johnny Zaro and Buddy Alcorn Mercs, and most recently the Harry Westergard 1941 Cad convertible. So you might think this 1932 Ford roadster is a bit out of character, but one reason Kurt was interested in it was because much of the custom work on the car was performed by famed Valley Custom for its first owner, Bill Hook, between 1949 and 1951.

As you can see, the body is deeply channeled, a Du Vall V-windshield has been molded to the cowl, and the rear pan has been rolled with vertical 1949 Ford lights installed. Less obvious are such things as hidden door hinges, custom dash, and "stepped" rear frame with reworked rear wheelwells. No one seems sure of how or why, but before the car was completed Hook sold it to Dr. Leland Wetzel of Springfield, Missouri, who finished the car there with a three-carb Evans-equipped flathead V-8, Jeepster yellow paint, dark-green pleated upholstery, and plenty of chrome including hefty nerf bars with the doctor's initial in front.

I don't have to tell you much more about this well-known roadster, because it received plenty of press after Wetzel finished it and he and his wife (along with another couple in their roadster) drove from Missouri to the Bonneville Nationals in 1952, where it was photographed for both *Hot Rod* and *Hop Up* magazines (including a familiar photo of the Wetzels sitting in it, checking out the SoCal belly tank). The story in the December 1952 *Hot Rod* magazine, was a classic written by Mrs. Wetzel, recounting their cross-country trip in a roadster "with no top, no fenders, and no heater." There was another two-page feature on the car in the small, East Coast *Custom Rodder* magazine in October 1958. But by October 1971, when a single photo of it appeared in a column in *Hot Rod* magazine, the caption read "owner unknown."

Well, Kurt and his wife, Amy, live just south of St. Louis in Missouri, and Springfield isn't that far away. He wondered if the good doctor might still have his well-traveled roadster. Leland Wetzel is not a common name, and he's a doctor besides. Actually, Kurt had heard from a friend who lived in the area, years before, that Wetzel still had the car. So it wasn't hard to find his address. Instead of calling, Kurt sent a very brief and polite letter, just before Christmas in 1993, inquiring if the doctor might be interested in selling the car and making an offer of a specified amount (he also mentioned he owned the restored *Dream Truck* and enclosed a photo). Dr. Wetzel promptly replied that "My 1932 is up on stands to keep the weight off the running gear. I am interested in selling the car," adding, "I want to see your truck." And so the deal was done.

The roadster was last licensed in 1970. The photos show how it looked in Dr. Wetzel's garage in Springfield where Kurt first saw it in early 1994, including the yellow paint, green upholstery, and the original flathead with Hellings decals still on the air cleaners. In the photo with the car outside for the first time in 25 years, Dr. Wetzel is the man on the right in the blue shirt.

When Kurt got the car home, it was in such good original condition that he simply cleaned it up, got it running again, and drove it as-is for a couple of years. However, Kurt really likes to restore his

historically significant cars to concours condition, even though he also likes to drive them a lot. Also, he suffers incurably from the (largely psychological) disease, Fear of Flatheads. So, after pulling the car completely apart, stripping it down to the original cherry sheetmetal and Valley Custom lead (plus pages of a 1944 *Los Angeles Times* stuffed in the doors and decklid), he had the car repainted by Dave Conrad and otherwise fully restored, except that in place of the flathead he substituted a very period-correct, S.Co.T.-supercharged early Cadillac overhead engine.

In the final photo, showing Kurt and a friend in the finished car, I don't know why Kurt doesn't look happier, because the restoration is otherwise perfect, down to the wide whites and chromed full-moon wheelcovers.

Johnny Taylor's Royal Coach

ongtime L.A. Roadsters member and proprietor of Verne's Chrome Plating in Gardena, California, Bob Barnes, told me about this purple Metalflake custom 1958 Ford two or three years ago. When he took me over to see it in nearby Hawthorne, it was in a small wood-frame one-car garage, behind an equally small house, where it was hard to see the car's details under a dim, single light bulb. The car's owner, Chris Yates, told me how he had to paint it, including multiple layers of Metalflake, plus purple and lavender candies and clear, in the driveway, because there wasn't enough room to spray paint in the garage.

Chris works in construction. When I went back recently to photograph the car, he had completely rebuilt the garage into a new master bedroom and attached it to the house, leaving this beautiful custom to sit in what's left of the driveway, outside, as you can see in one of the photos. At least he keeps it covered.

Of course I remembered the car very well from the May 1963 cover of *Rod & Custom*, when it was owned by Johnny Taylor and built by Art Lehner and son of the Art Chrome body shop in Hollydale, a small L.A. suburb just east of Lynwood. Although it wasn't chopped, channeled, or sectioned, this car was stunning for its two shades of purple Metalflake, its all-chrome three-carb 390 engine, and especially its sculptured white-pearl-and-purple-frieze interior by

Harry Loveland with four T-Bird bucket seats, a bar and ice chest in the rear, a TV in the dash, and a record player and telephone in the center console. Of course the trunk was done to match.

Custom accents included functional scoops in the roof and deck lid, extended fins, eight 1959 Cad taillights in molded housings, recessed and hooded headlights, a 1959 Imperial grille, and 1953 Stude lower pans front and rear. Extra points-getters included the

dual handmade sidepipes coming through the front fenders, and especially the 800 small, chromed studs machined by Taylor in high school shop class and attached in very neat rows on a gold background inside the stock side chrome. Further enhancing its looks, the car sat about 2 inches off the ground on chrome-reversed rims with 1960 Ford hubcaps. Johnny bought the car new in 1958. It was prevalent on the SoCal show scene for a couple years in the early 1960s, and then poof! It was gone.

Chris Yates had no idea what it was when he got it. He was a 17-year-old in high school in Manhattan Beach in 1984, driving a 1970 SS Camaro, when he saw an ad for a custom 1950 Ford with a Carson top on a lot in San Diego, and he liked the look. He and his mom drove down with the intention to buy the 1950, but it was a piece of junk with 2x4s in place of springs. But on the same lot—nobody knows when or how it got there—was this 1958 Ford looking much like it did on the *Rod & Custom* cover in 1963. Chris traded his Camaro and $1,000 he borrowed from his mom for the car, and drove it home, with the pipes scraping on every dip and his mother worrying that he was going to become "one of those lowriders."

Well, there was nothing like this in his high school parking lot in the 1980s, to be sure, and everybody loved it. But for Chris, who was (and still is) a muscle car guy, it was daily transportation, so he started by raising it up enough to drive. Then, pretty soon, the lacquer paint went away and he repainted it white, and then black. It had 22,000 original miles on it when he got it, and he soon added another 30,000. After 10 years it was tired, so he parked it to build more muscular street machines.

Eventually, Chris came to appreciate what the car was and decided to restore it. Johnny Taylor is gone, but Chris was able to contact a son and a daughter, who had some early photos (one is shown here), but not much more information on the car. The daughter said her father sold it to one of her high school friends around 1975. How it got to San Diego is a mystery.

Chris has done most of the restoration on the car himself, on a limited budget. The engine is the same 390 Taylor installed in 1962. Of course the interior was a major job and, unfortunately, the car sat in one shop for a number of years with nothing getting done. Fortunately, Chris was able to retrieve it and got Joe Perez to do the wonderful job you see here. I wish I could show more of this car's details, inside and out, because there are so many. This one is a lucky survivor.

"One Just Like It" Deuce Roadster

Remember I mentioned that you could use one hot rod as bait to find another? Here's an example of that with a slight twist. The story starts at the L.A. Roadsters show swap meet a couple years ago.

Derek Bower and his friend Carpo had taken a very rusty, but very original and complete 1932 Ford roadster to the swap to sell. With a big price tag, they were fishing. They didn't expect what they caught.

Of course the car didn't sell, and Derek was loading it back on the trailer Sunday afternoon when a guy wandered up and said, "I know where there's one just like that." Derek said, "What kind?" Guy: "That's a 1932 Ford, right? One of those." Derek: "What body style?" Guy: "Like that, a convertible with no top." Derek: "Tell me about it." Guy: "It's a friend's. It's in his garage; he's moving and he wants to sell it."

Including the rusty one on the trailer, Derek had been through plenty of these hunts, so he was skeptical. The guy took Derek's number, said he'd talk to the owner, and call back. Well, Derek heard nothing and forgot about it. But then the guy called. Derek was still doubtful it was a 1932 Ford. The guy said, "Do you have email? I'll send some pictures." He did, and it was a 1932 Ford. A very cherry-looking 1932 hiboy roadster from way back, in fact. Derek was there the next day.

Long story short: The owner's grandfather was a house painter working at the home of a Hollywood producer in 1947 or 1948 and this roadster was sitting in the driveway, much the way it looks now. The producer said, "It's my son's but he doesn't like it. Do you want to buy it?" So granddad bought it, painted it tan, and drove it until he got a fender ticket in 1952. He

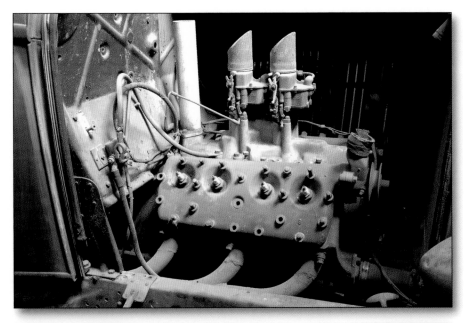

the roadster running, sprayed some gray primer on it, and drove it up and down the block one time before parking it again. In 1959 the family moved to Lakewood, where the roadster was flat-towed, parked in the garage, and forgotten. Grampa was long gone; the guy's father had now passed away and the son was getting ready to sell the house.

Now this isn't like the coupe that could've been had for $550 (on page 126). When Derek asked how much, the guy said, "I've been to a couple of shows and people are asking $35,000 for these." Derek could only nod in agreement, especially considering what he was asking for his rusty one a few weeks before. Then the owner said, "I know this one needs to be completely redone. I'd like to get $22,000." Derek couldn't help noticing that the rafters were full of 1940 Ford parts: fenders, doors, hoods, running boards. The owner said he'd like to sell all that, too. So Derek asked if he'd throw it in for the price. The deal was struck.

So this one wasn't cheap. But it was nearly perfect. You can see one dime-size rust hole in the floor. That's it. It was never hit. The only thing missing is the seat (the windshield is in the trunk). The rear pan has never been cut (it had trailer lights bolted on the frame horns). It still has the gennie gauges and the rubber floor mats! It has a very early dropped axle, and the mechanical brakes were later converted to hydraulic with a Bell Auto kit. The 1934 21-stud engine has a big cam of some sort and a rare Thickstun PM-7 intake with two once-chromed 94 carbs. The only other mod is a 1946 Merc steering wheel.

The patina on this car is incredible, but I'm afraid it exists only in photos. Given that Derek has a nice Hemi-powered 1932 roadster of his own that only needs paint and upholstery to finish, plus the rusty one, he couldn't afford to keep this find. It's now at Brizio's being built into a fine street rod. But the point is that these cars are out there, sitting in garages in suburbs like Lakewood.

bolted some bobbed Model A fenders on the rear, but got another ticket for no front fenders, and parked the car in disgust in 1953. That's the last time it was registered, as you can see from the plate.

By 1957 his grandson turned 16, and (without his father's permission or knowledge) he and a friend got

The Candy-and-Chrome 1940

When I first saw this 1940 DeLuxe coupe at Paso Robles in 2004 or 2005, what drew my attention was the Olds engine. The car appeared to be red suede, and nothing else about it looked special. Then I noticed the firewall. It was crusty with rust, but it had been chromed. Now, you have to understand that the firewall doesn't come out of a 1940 Ford. It's permanently attached with about 100 spot welds. To get it out, chrome it, and get it back in without ruining it is nearly impossible. I was pondering this when the owner, Mike Aahl, said, "Look underneath." The entire frame was chromed! I've seen a million hot rods, but I'd never seen a 1940 Ford with a chrome firewall or frame. So then Mike, who's a talkative guy and who'd driven it down from Hayward, across the bay from San Francisco, told me the story.

Mike is a used-car broker and has a large, old garage full of rods, customs, and memorabilia. He says he's been "playing with cars about 40 years, hobby cars." One you might recognize behind the 1940 is a "dual-cowl" 1936 Ford Phaeton with two Du Vall windshields, which he's owned about 30 years. But the candy-red '40 with the chrome frame and undercarriage was right in his hometown for decades and he never knew it. Of course he knew the car—everybody in the area did.

Advanced Plating in Oakland had to build special tanks to chrome that frame. The bill reputedly came to $6,800 (in the 1960s) for everything under the car and hood that could be plated.

The sign in the show photo says the car was torn apart in 1960 and took six years to complete. But it doesn't say who painted or upholstered it. I can see that it won a couple of other trophies. But records indicate it was shown at Oakland only once, in 1967, when thisphoto was taken. It belonged to Ed and Fran Leite, who lived

six blocks from Mike's current garage. Fran still lives there. She remembers the car well, but she has no idea where it went when Ed left and took it with him.

About five years ago one of Mike's relatives was having a family party in Union City, about 10 miles south. On his way down, Mike's son spotted a stock, green Forty parked between two houses a couple blocks away, with grass growing up to the bumpers. He told his dad, and they took off to see it. A young guy in the house said it wasn't for sale, but his sister had one that was. He didn't know much else, but said it was a hot rod and thought it had a flathead, and it was in a shop where they were trying to get it to run. He took Mike's number and said he'd call with the info, but Mike wasn't too interested, figuring it must be a piece of junk.

The story gets complicated, but Leite had died, leaving one 1940 to his son and the other to his daughter, both of whom were clueless flakes, in Mike's estimation. But, a month later, the son did call with the name of the shop. Mike went there, and had to climb over about 50 cars to get to the 1940, which was at the back with its hood up. He was thinking this was crazy, as he was banging his shins on bumpers. But when he finally saw the three carbs, the Olds engine, and then that firewall, he stopped in his tracks. He suddenly realized it was the one with the chrome frame.

The radiator, generator, and gas tank were missing, all of which I assume were chrome. The shop had done no further work, and was owed money. Somebody had supposedly offered $13,000 for it. Mike figured he'd better move fast, so he dealt with the second wife, secured the red car (and its pink slip), and eventually got the green one, too.

There's more to the story, including the fact that several of Mike's buddies knew about the green stocker in the grass, but hadn't asked about it—and certainly didn't know about the red one connected to it—so they thought Mike "stole them." Goes to show: Ask.

All Mike had to do was put a radiator, gas tank, and generator in the car to get it running. The engine is perfect. The white upholstery is nearly so. The chrome took a month and a half of hand polishing to get it to look as good as it does. The chrome wheels and Royal Master tires were still on it, but Mike uses the ones shown for driving. Unfortunately, the candy-red lacquer is crazed and won't polish, but makes a nice shade of suede. And that's just how Mike is going to keep it. Serendipity is how, and where, you find it.

The Deuce in the Driveway

For starters, here's one that's almost unbelievable. But not only is it true, I even have photos. The story goes like this: Larry Gimenez and Bill Stecker are long-time members of the L.A. Roadsters club, and they both happen to live in San Pedro. A friend of Stecker's young son moved to Lakewood, not far away, and the son goes to visit him. Knowing that his dad likes old cars, the friend tells Stecker's son that the old lady next door (to the house they've recently moved into) has an old car in her driveway that she'd like to get rid of. Nobody knows what it is, other than an "old car." It turns out the lady is 92 years old, the car belonged to her son, and the son is in the hospital, mortally ill.

How's that for a setup? Let me interject that Lakewood is the Levittown of L.A. It includes several square miles of small tract homes built in the late 1940s just after the war. Many were bought by young, returning GIs to start raising families. So today, many are still owned by the same people, who are now quite old, and their garages are full of a long life's worth of "stuff." And those who have moved into the sprawling suburban neighborhood since then are primarily blue-collar types who tend to work on, and fix up, their own cars. In other words, this is exactly the type of place where you should be hunting for vintage tin and hidden old hot rods.

So Stecker's son comes home and tells his dad about the old car. Knowing it's probably a piece of junk, Bill says he doesn't have time, so he tells Gimenez about it. Larry's retired, and builds cars in his garage, and Lakewood isn't that far away, so he says, "Why not?" This is a Friday afternoon.

Larry meets the lady and one of her other sons who's there to help her clean out the yard, and she says, yes, she wants to get rid of the "old car." So Larry goes to the side of the house, they open these big wooden gates in the driveway, and there sits a near-complete, near-virgin 1932 Ford three-window coupe! The V-8 engine is missing, the hood and radiator are off (but they're there), the fenders are dented, and the thing is all patina'd, but otherwise it's mint.

Larry, as casually as possible, asks how much she wants. The lady hesitates and says, "Well, we have an offer already." So Larry thinks, "Uh oh, here it comes," and asks how much. She says $500. Undoubtedly too eagerly, Larry replies, "I'll give you $1,000." The lady says "OK" and the son agrees. Of course Larry has to come back with a hauler (and some roller wheels/tires, which you see in the photos) the next day. But before he leaves he pulls out all the cash he has on him, about $300, and gives it to the son to make sure this gem will really be there when he comes back.

He does and it is. When he gets it home to his garage and starts stripping it, he can't believe how cherry it is. The firewall and frame are perfect; there are no dents in the body; and the only rust is one small spot in the trunk floor where the back window leaked. As the garage photos show, this car took very little to block out and prep for gorgeous black paint.

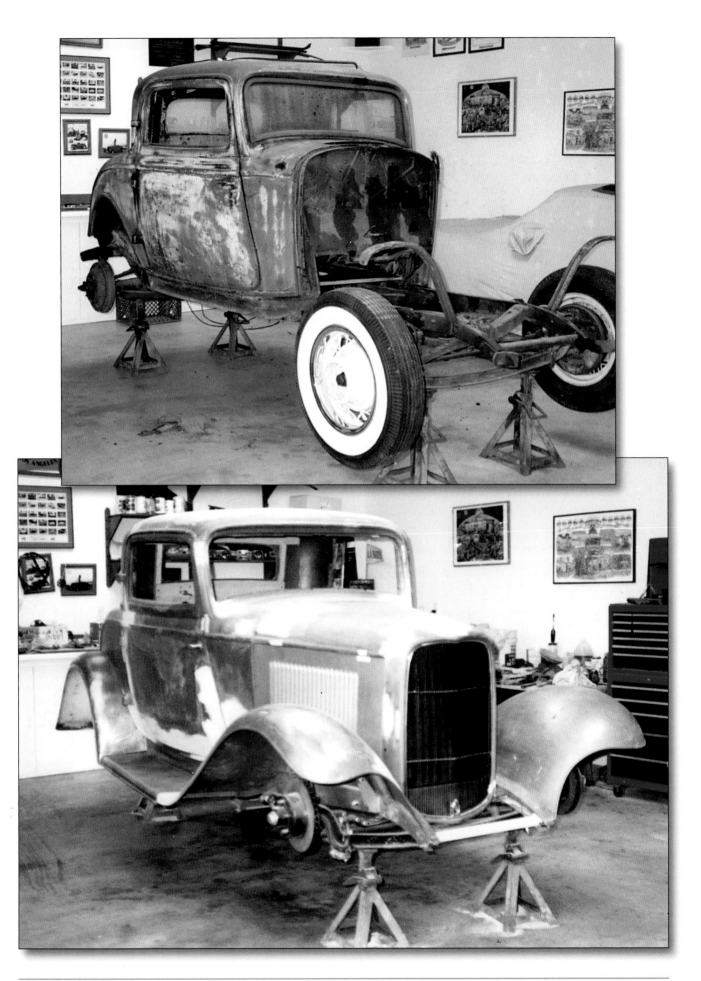

Larry had someone else fill the roof, but otherwise he built it into a striking, simple, "blacked out" street rod with Pete & Jake's chassis components, small-block Ford power, and medium-tan leather interior by Lanny Boetl.

Larry's hot rod friend and neighbor, Alex Carresi, also retired, came over to help with much of the body prep and construction. So after Larry enjoyed driving the car extensively for a couple of years, but was ready to start on a new 1932 sedan delivery project, he offered to sell the car to Alex for "what he had in it," which was quite fair. So the now-beautiful black Deuce that came from the old lady's driveway now sits in Alex's garage, next to his black-and-flamed 1934, and both get driven plenty.

But here's the clincher. He got the car about 10 years ago, and Larry still kicks himself that, "I'm sure I could have gotten it for $550." OK, but get this, "And there's another one right on the other side of my back fence." Yep. Larry says he saw it in 1982 when he was building his garage, and he figures it was there at least 10 years before that. It's another complete, rust-free, full-fendered 1932 three-window. Larry says he's gone over to ask the guy repeatedly to sell it, and he just says no. So it's still sitting there right now. Hey, some you win, some you don't (at least not yet).

The Graffiti Impala

Regardless of your age, you've all seen *American Graffiti* at least two or three times by now. And if you've gone to an indoor car show anywhere in the country in the last 20 years, you've probably seen the yellow 1932 coupe that was one of the stars of the movie, with one or two of the lesser stars there signing glossy photos, because Rick Figari has been touring it incessantly around the world since he bought it as a 20-year-old in 1985.

And you might have read an article or two about the black 1955 Chevy. I should make that plural, because there were three of them: two big-block, 4-speed, true street racers built for the movie *Two-Lane Blacktop,* one of which was painted glossy for *American Graffiti,* plus the crash-scene car, which ended up on a circle track because of its roll cage.

I'm not sure exactly where the *Graffiti* '55 is at this moment, but the other black-primer *Blacktop* '55 was stolen from the Universal lot right after that movie wrapped, and may have turned up on the East Coast just recently. The chopped Merc? Guitarist/ singer Brian Setzer got it, made it look as good as he could, then sold it to a guy in Plainview, New York, in 1987, as seen in the August 1991 issue of *Rod & Custom.*

That leaves the 1958 Impala with the tuck-and-roll interior that was owned by the Ron Howard character but was driven by the Toad during most of the movie. That one has been "lost" since I reported on all the cars in the May 1976 issue of *Street Rodder* magazine. But I've known where it's been all along. Its story is as good as any in this book.

Mike Famalette grew up in Vallejo, which is at the northeast end of the San Francisco Bay, less than 40 miles from Petaluma, where the film was shot. But Mike didn't know anything about the movie. It wasn't released yet. He was a 17-year-old senior in high school in 1972 and was looking for his first car. So when he saw an ad in the *San Francisco Chronicle* for "1958 Chevy Impala, tuck-and-roll, $325," he was interested. The ad also listed a 1951 Merc for $975, a 1932 Ford coupe for $200 (a typo; they meant $2,000), and a 1955 Chevy for $2,000, among others. (Remember, nobody knew if this movie would make it, let alone be a hit, at this point.) All the cars were in nearby Sonoma, in the backyard of Henry Travers, the transportation manager of the film. So young Mike called and went to look. A mild custom 1958 Impala with tuck-and-roll, 1959 Caddy bullet taillights, and red fogged paint over white was not a cool high

school car in 1972. In fact, Mike says he would have bought the 1955 Chevy if he could have afforded it, but it was way too much.

The 1958 had a tired 348 in it, with a 3-speed trans, and Mike had never driven a stick shift before. So when he tried to test-drive it, it didn't go too well. Plus they had quickly shaved the door handles for the movie, but didn't install solenoids, so you had to leave the windows open to get in (the driver's window was cracked during filming because someone didn't). But Mike was hungry to get his first car, and this one was cool, in its way. He offered $275. They wouldn't take it. So he paid $285 and drove it home. It was the only car that sold. They didn't even mention the name of the movie, and Mike didn't ask.

When he got it home, he found a Tri-Power intake with two of the carbs in the trunk. There was a single 4-barrel on the engine, which was a smoker. So Mike and his older brother Jose swapped in a 283 and a Powerglide. Remember, this was Mike's high school cruiser, his first and only car at the time. But he knew he'd want to put the original driveline back in at some point, so anything they took off they saved, bagged, and labeled. They also did other work to make the car safe and drivable, but they didn't change anything on it. It still has no solenoids in the doors.

But then, just a few months after this work was done, *American Graffiti* came to the local theater, and Mike soon learned that was the movie his car was in. So, for fun, he and some buddies got in the car and cruised up and down the main drag, in front of the theater, as it let out that Saturday night. Can you imagine? These guys were seniors in high school! It was very much like the movie, only this was real.

After the movie became a smash hit and cultural touchstone, Mike knew he'd keep the car forever and

preserve it as best he could. Remember, movie cars are "50-footers" at best, and treated very roughly on the set, so this was no show car to start with. And Mike's had it 37 years. He hasn't over-restored anything, but its condition remains amazingly good. He says it still has 1972 air in the back tires, and his wife recently found correct front replacements (E78-14 Kelly Springfields) on eBay. Best of all, their daughter Ashley installed the original 348 (rebuilt locally), with the matching Tri-Power, as her senior high school project a couple years ago, and got a deserved A grade for the job. The car has a Turbo 350 transmission in it now, but the clutch pedal has remained in the car all along (beside the Eelco foot-shaped gas pedal), and Mike is prepping the 3-speed to go back in.

Mike spent a stint in the Marines in SoCal after high school, then a career with a utility company in the North Bay until retiring recently to some rural acreage in northeastern Washington, about 40 miles from the Canadian border. He of course has been an excellent custodian of the Impala all this time, and we have remained in touch, so my wife and I were happy to be able to drive up and pay a visit to Mike and the Chevy on our vacation last summer, where the accompanying photos were taken.

So the *American Graffiti* 1958 Impala isn't lost at all. It's been in Mike Famalette's garage all this time, well appreciated and cared for. He bought it as his first car, his high school cruiser, for $285 nearly 40 years ago. His daughter reinstalled the original Tri-Power 348 as her high school senior project. It's got 1972 air in the tires and tuck-and-roll older than that. This story is amazing. It would make a good movie.

Lost and Found

I mentioned earlier that the most incongruous of lost-and-found hot rods are race cars, especially dragsters. An outdated dragster is worth less than a 10-year-old Cadillac. Not only does nobody want it, but it's invariably illegal to run anymore. Plus, as stated, dragsters are long, gangly things that you're always tripping over in the garage or shop. They take up a lot of room. How in the world have so many survived?

"Reunion" drag meets started 10 to 15 years ago, and every year more wonderful, often beautiful, Top Fuel dragsters and other long-forgotten drag machines show up, as if they're crawling out of the woodwork. Admittedly, many of these cars, today, are mostly reconstructed from a few bits and pieces of the original car (if any). But, since there are so many of these dragsters to see (and hear!) today, I've chosen just a select few to show here because of their historicity, their originality, or because they have such good stories to tell.

Chapter Seven

Horsepower Engineering

Doug Robinson's Horsepower Engineering in Pasadena, California, makes tubular headers. Today he specializes primarily in Porsche applications, but it's a local hot rod institution. Just a block off of famed Colorado Boulevard, it's been there for decades. Doug, besides being one of the nicest people I know, is one of those few mechanical wizards who can design and build anything. And he can make engines—whether they are ancient GMC sixes with home-brewed superchargers, flatheads, Chevys, or venerable Chrysler Hemis on big loads of nitromethane—do things most others can't. He holds so many records at Bonneville and El Mirage, in a plethora of classes, that I don't have the room to even list them here. And he's planning how to get more right now.

Doug started out drag racing in the 1960s. He built two dragsters before learning two lessons: If you want your picture in *Drag News* or the magazines, paint it a bright color; and if you want to go fast, put a blown Chrysler Hemi in it and feed it nitro. That's

what he did in 1963 when he built this swoopy 150-inch rail. When I say "he built," I mean he built it himself. He ran it until 1966, mainly in SoCal, which had plenty of tracks in those days: Pomona, Fontana, Irwindale, Lions, with a few trips up to Fremont or out to Arizona. The car (with Doug driving) won its share of weekend Top Eliminators at all these tracks, turning a best of 7.43 at 208 mph. But he didn't tour, chase points, or win any major meets. The car did, however, get a deserved two-page spread in the August 1965 issue of *Rod & Custom*, among other mags.

But this car has two claims to fame. First, it was sponsored by KRLA radio, one of the biggest rock-and-roll stations in the nation, with the hottest DJs, during that heyday of rock-and-roll AM radio. How Doug got that sponsorship, what it entailed, and what he had to do to fulfill it is a big story in itself, which I'll have to tell when I have more space. But the truly important part is that this was one of the first, big, non-automotive entities to sponsor, and have its name painted on, a Top Fuel dragster. It even

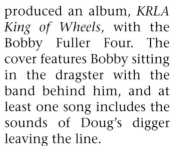

produced an album, *KRLA King of Wheels*, with the Bobby Fuller Four. The cover features Bobby sitting in the dragster with the band behind him, and at least one song includes the sounds of Doug's digger leaving the line.

Second, this dragster was one of the very few to ever beat the awesome Greer-Black-Prudhomme rail. It happened at Fontana, Doug's "home" track. They were using a new system whereby the starter rested the tip of his flag on a button, starting the clocks as he lifted the flag. Prudhomme thought he had this timed, but Doug had raced against this methodical starter more often, and knew that he could leave as soon as the starter twitched his shoulder. Doug gated Prudhomme by a car length, and won with a slightly slower ET—but he won. And Prudhomme still remembers it.

Doug sold the car in 1966 when it was still No. 2 on the *Drag News* Top Fuel list. The new owner asked Doug to drive the car in the next big race, and the engine blew so badly it bent the frame. The car never ran again. Doug figured it got scrapped. But in 1978 his son unexpectedly found it, in pieces, in a shop or yard in Ontario, California. The engine was gone, the frame was still bent, but it was otherwise mostly there, including the original paint and lettering.

Doug bought it, repaired the frame, put it back together with a dummy motor, and held a team reunion party in 1979. After that, he hung the entire car up on the wall of his shop, above the pipe racks, and it stayed right there for the next 25 years. But with the "cacklefest" and reunion activity happening, he figured it was time to get it down and spruce it up. The body and paint is still gennie to 1966. The engine in it in the photos is a dummy, but Doug has a new runner screwed together, on a stand, ready to drop in. And he has plenty of nitro.

Tom Prufer's Red Rail

Tom Prufer has done the things most hot rodders dream about. He's had outstanding, class-winning coupes, roadsters, or dragsters in nearly every Oakland Roadster Show since the mid 1950s. He's had several cars on the covers of magazines, most notably the sliced, diced, and flamed fenderless '33 known as *Cop Shop Coupe*. But one of Tom's first and most enduring loves is drag racing—notably nitromethane-fueled drag racing, both in front-engine rails and rear-engine roadsters (*a la* Speed Sport). He's never been eminently successful at it; he just loves doing it—everything about it. In fact he just premiered a new/old cacklefest digger at this year's Reunion at Bakersfield.

Undoubtedly Tom's major legacy, and triumph, in drag racing was initiating the first Nostalgia Nationals drags (with partner Brian Burnett) at Fremont Raceway in 1981. This was the beginning of the whole nostalgia drags/reunion phenomenon that continues so strongly today. Of course, back then, we could actually run our old, refurbished drag cars down the track. I say "we" because I was actively and eagerly involved in this racing, running an Altered roadster and then a Top Fuel dragster.

And, besides running the events, Tom found time to put together and run his own blown Chrysler TE-440 rail. So neither of us noticed (I think it was 1985) when this guy drove into the pits with an old red, short-wheelbase dragster, complete less engine, on the back of a flatbed truck. I certainly didn't get any pictures of it. But someone who saw it, and recognized it, found Tom and said, "I think your old dragster just showed up." Tom was flabbergasted. He hadn't seen this car since the mid 1960s. But it was his car—the most successful one he had. The guy who brought it in had no clue about what it was, and I

never have been able to find out where or how he got it. Obviously trying not to look too excited, Tom made a deal to buy the car, telling the guy to "drop it off in my driveway," which he did. But let's back up....

Tom is from the Bay Area, but he got into dragsters when he was stationed in Tucson while in the Air Force. A local racer named John Patrick had a successful fuel rail called *Power King*, and he built race car chassis. So Tom had Patrick build the basics of this car (being Tom's second or third dragster), and called it

Power King Too. However, it wasn't until he was back home that he had Bay Area drag legend Romeo Palamides form the swoopy, louvered, red-painted, and Greek-striped body.

With an Enderle injector and scoop on top of a pruned 6-71 blower on top of a "small" 354-inch Chrysler Hemi, Tom began running this car in 1960. The first photo here shows the car (with Rich Guasco's AMBR-winning roadster behind it) at the 1961 Oakland Roadster Show, where it won first in its class. But it did just as well on the track. The second photo, showing its characteristic profile, was taken at the Redding, California, track, where it not only ran 179-mph/8.50-second times (and was proclaimed "World's Fastest 354 Chrysler"), but was also photographed for a two-page feature that ran in the March 1963 *Rod & Custom*.

Tom finally sold the car in 1963 to Chuck Flores, who reputedly won Top Eliminator with it at Half Moon Bay drag strip for several weeks in a row, continuing to run the car a few more years. Where it went after that is a mystery.

But when Tom got the car back, he immediately set about fully restoring it. The third photo shows Tom (in the funny glasses) warming the car on the line at Fremont in 1986 or 1987 with its original driver Bob "Jet Car" Smith at the wheel. In the final photo Tom himself is in the car on a very hot summer weekend in Oklahoma City, where it ran for the last time. Such vintage dragsters were soon banned by the NHRA from actually running down the track. So Tom ultimately decided to donate this one to Don Garlits' Museum of Drag Racing in Ocala, Florida, where you can see it on display today.

The Alcala T

Other than Art Chrisman's venerable No. 25 dragster, I can't think of any other running/runnable drag car today that has more history than this one. What's more significant and amazing, however, is that this one has never been restored.

The story is a bit fuzzy about this 1923 T's origins. The car belonged to Creighton Hunter, the owner of Hunter Oil Company in Santa Ana, and one of the founding partners of the Santa Ana drag strip. But I don't know who originally built it, or for what specific purpose. I know Creighton ran it at the dry lakes, because there are a couple of photos of it there, unpainted and wearing the number "96 C." However, especially with the nerf bars front and rear, the belly-pan/footwell, the tonneau cover, center steering, and even the upswept pipes, it has the definite appearance of a circle-track roadster typical of the latter 1940s. Even the 1932 Plymouth tubular front axle was a popular track item. The most unusual part of the car is the cut-down 1937 Ford pickup grille shell, which I've never seen used as a track T nose, but it works quite well, doesn't it? The problem is I don't know who made it, along with the three-piece aluminum hood with five air scoops.

These are things I could have asked Creighton, but didn't, and now he's gone. The other big question, of course, is what was the derivation of those eyeballs on the side of the car? One story I seem to remember had something to do with fried eggs, sunny-side up, but that may be apocryphal. What is fact is that this red paint, the lettering, even the decals, and that yellow "00" number with the eyes inside were all applied right around the time the Santa Ana track opened in 1950. This was well before Dean Moon came up with his Mooneyes logo, but it might be where he got the idea.

More important than all this, however, is the fact that Creighton Hunter only owned this roadster for a short time, and didn't even run it at Santa Ana that often. He was busy trying to sort out a strange, wedge-shaped, three-wheel dragster called *Flying Piece of Pie*,

which ultimately crashed (but also had the "00" eyeball number on it). So he sold the red roadster to Hill Alcala in 1952, and it was he and his family who ran the car very successfully at Santa Ana and most other SoCal tracks. Racers such as the Berardini brothers and Dale Lambrose (Iacono Roadster) remember this Alcala roadster well because it was often the hardest to beat (if they even could).

If you're a magazine collector, and you've seen this car in early issues, it is a true time warp because it simply hasn't changed. It first appeared on the cover of the April 1955 *Rod & Custom*, shown from the rear being flagged off at Santa Ana. It was also on the cover of *Rodding and Restyling*, March 1956. The most telling is a two-page spread in the October 1961 *Hot Rod*. There it wears Moon wheelcovers in the static photos, but in a shot of it leaving the line it has the same mag wheels on the back seen in today's photos. The engine photos are virtually identical: same manifold, carbs, heads, magneto, and even water hoses/tank. And, to demonstrate a definite connection between this car

and Moon, the article states that Hill was tapped to be the first driver of the *Mooneyes* dragster, which made its debut on the prior *Hot Rod* cover.

Hill continued running the roadster with success, setting a track record at the Riverside 1/4-mile at 133 mph in the low 10s, on fuel. But running the car was always a family affair, and Hill turned the wheel over to his son, Tony, in the mid 1960s. Of course classes for this type of car waned until the advent of vintage drags. The action photo shows Tony storming off the line at OCIR at the Antique Nationals in 1980 (with the grille cover unusually off), where the car won its class three years in a row, and has competed regularly.

In the 1990s, Tony leaned on the car pretty hard, racing at various nostalgia meets such as NDRA, ANRA, and Goodguys, winning various eliminator brackets, pulling impressive wheels-up launches, breaking the venerable quick-change (leading to a 9-inch rear swap, as well as a mandated roll cage), and impressive 10.80-second/120-mph times on gasoline. Unfortunately, Tony passed away unexpectedly after the 1994 season, so the car has been passed down to his son, Tony, Jr., and it has been retired, more or less. At least Tony took the roll cage out, and now plans to reinstall the Halibrand Q.C. But that's all that really needs to be done, because nothing else on the car has changed since 1950. And the Alcala family intends to keep it that way.

The Wrapped Dragster

Remember that stack of names and numbers of "to find" cars I mentioned that I've always kept next to my phone? This one sat in that stack for two years before I finally acted on it. That was in 1987, and I briefly reported on it in *Hot Rod* magazine. I'll paraphrase what I wrote, because this story is just as amazing now as it was then. This one was almost like literally unwrapping a mummy found in a long-lost pharaoh's tomb.

Somebody had mentioned in passing that a blown Chrysler early dragster was stored in someone's backyard in the high desert above L.A., and gave me a name and a number. Not only was there supposed to be a complete dragster, but a virgin 1932 Ford coupe as well. This sounded too good to be true, but I kept the number. A couple years later I was in the area, so I thought I'd call. The guy who answered was Tony Moise and,

yes, he had a very virgin 1932 five-window sitting in his garage (as you see in the photo), complete and original other than a dropped axle and juice brakes. It'd been there 20-plus years. But the dragster was over at his former partner Chuck Hulsizer's house, stored under wraps in the backyard. I was still dubious.

When we got there, sure enough, there was something looking like a mummified rail up against a brick wall, wrapped in plastic and canvas. When Chuck cut the steel straps, the canvas fell away, rotted. Underneath was the most complete, beautiful, period-perfect early dragster I had ever seen in original and unrestored condition. It was a classic, muffler-moly, Chassis Research TE-440 purchased from Scotty Fenn in 1959.

The 392 Hemi had long, upswept chrome headers and a complete Potvin front-drive 6-71 with a two-port Hilborn injector and a custom, candy-red scoop. The alternate Isky top-mount blower, manifold, and drive were also wrapped and stored in the garage. It had Lyle Fisher–laced spoke wheels in the front and Halibrand mags with hand-lettered M&H Racemasters in back. Parts of a dual-disc clutch sat in the bottom

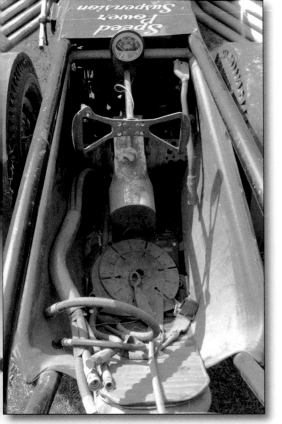

of the black tuck-and-roll seat. And the candy-red paint was cracked, but not faded.

It was obviously a good-looking car in its day. It even posted some pretty good Top Gas times up at the Inyokern track, in the still-higher desert where the air is really thin. But it never raced much anywhere else, and certainly didn't make a name for itself.

Then, sometime in the mid 1960s, it broke a cylinder sleeve in a block that had obviously been repaired before, so Tony and Chuck decided to park it. And wrap it. In fact, after I took the accompanying photos in 1987, they wrapped it back up again and it sat there another 13 years.

Somehow they learned about long-time (and current) drag racer and collector of many things, Jim Burskin, of Redding in far-north California. There, on several acres, he has developed his Museum of Historical Rust that includes everything from a complete carousel and operating steam train to vintage farm machinery and all sorts of race cars and other vehicles and memorabilia. The color photo shows the dragster on display in one of the buildings, cleaned and polished, but still unrestored in any way. It's been on loan there since about 2000. It still has the broken sleeve in the engine (for now).

Oh yes, that virgin 1932 coupe in Tony's garage? It took him a while, but it's finally bright red, finished, and probably out on the road right now with Tony driving it somewhere.

Doug Cook's 1937 Chevy

Doug Cook, as in Stone, Woods, and Cook, started his illustrious drag-racing career in this 1937 Chevy coupe. If you know your drag-racing history, you undoubtedly know that Doug won the C/Gas class at the NHRA Nationals in Detroit in 1959, and set the C/GS record more than once, running a 4-71-blown Chevy engine built by Howard Johansen in this car. The next year Howard installed the blown Mouse in a 1940 Willys coupe, with Doug driving, and reset the C/GS record. Doug, of course, drove blue Willys coupes for several years after that, doing quite well. But he never got rid of that 1937 Chevy.

The old, very grainy photo shows a young Doug in the driver's seat of this car around 1957 or early 1958. It's hitched to the back of a nosed, decked, and pinstriped 1951 Olds 88, ready to tow to the strip. At that time it had three 97s on the Chevy engine. But if you squint, you can see that the 1937 looked more like a mild custom than a race car, with its wide whitewalls with 1955 Dodge Lancer wheelcovers, white upholstery on the stock bench seat, and rear license mounted on the bumper in a 1949 Chevy guard. Doug said it was painted Tahitian Red at the time, and

both cars even had Appleton spotlights. If you squint even harder, you might be able to see a dash full of Stewart-Warner and Sun gauges, and louvers in the hood top.

The hood louvers and gauges are still in the car. Also on the dash, besides white striping around the gauges, is a large tarantula serving up a big V-8 on a platter, with "Olds" written on one head and "Cad" on the other. This is signed "Flea 1957," who was a contemporary and competitor of Von Dutch. The white headliner, black piping, and chrome window frames are still there, too, but now the car has more race-like black individual seats.

Unfortunately, Doug is no longer with us to ask, but his son Mike says the 394 Olds engine now in the car is one that Doug won at some big meet with the S-W-C car; he can't remember exactly where or when. But it was installed in the 1937 around 1963 or 1964, along with a B&M stick hydro and a 5.13:1-geared 1957 Olds rear that were take-outs from the race Willys. Mainly because the car was so straight, they painted it black lacquer at this time, though you can see vestiges of the red on the firewall.

Mike says Doug drove the 1937 regularly, and he vividly remembers riding with him, after the Olds and hydro were installed, when they blew off one or two unsuspecting street "competitors." Since then Mike has installed more streetable gears in the rear, and the family keeps the car ready to drive. I took the accompanying photos in Mike, Jr.'s driveway about five years ago. The black paint is beginning to rub through in spots, but they're keeping this piece of true drag-racing history in fine shape.

Syndicate Scuderia

In the beginning dragsters were anything but pretty. And today, "beautiful" is the last word you'd use to describe a Top Fueler. But during the 1960s, front-engine rails were not only plentiful, many were really good looking. Favorites often include *Glass Slipper*, *Ernie's Camera*, the Ivo twin-Buick or *Barnstormer*, Gene Adams' *Shark Car*, Greer-Black-Prudhomme (of course), and then the lizard-nose cars like Stellings and Hampshire's.

I've already dated myself with that list, but one of my personal favorites has always been the mysterious *Syndicate Scuderia*. This A/Dragster showed up, seemingly out of nowhere (actually from Vancouver, Canada) at the 1963 Winternationals in Pomona. It had dark-blue candy paint with gold-leaf lettering, an equally dark-blue tinted canopy over the driver, a Chrysler Hemi with chrome weed-eater headers, and a front-driven 6-71 blower tucked inside the swoopy aluminum body. I saw the car run there (as seen in the first black-and-white photo) and it looked both beautiful and mean—snarky—at the same time, like a dashing masked bandit (i.e., Ramon Navarro as Zorro). It won Best Appearing Car at that meet. And then it was gone.

The 1963 Winternats was when the NHRA reinstated Top Fuel, and Gas Dragsters were dominated by twin-engine AA/Ds. There wasn't much incentive to run an A/D at national events anymore.

So Jack Williams and his team (the "Syndicate Scuderia") ran the car at local area tracks, soon mounting the blower on top to allow pulley changes, as seen in the second early photo. Jack, who still operates a fabrication/speed-parts shop by that name in the Vancouver area, said he started construction of this dragster on the shop floor in 1960, building the entire chassis, as well as the gas-welded aluminum body, himself. Always running gas, he competed until 1969, running a best of 8.40/187, and then hung the complete car, less engine, from the rafters of the shop. It stayed there until 1986, when he got it down, repainted it, and restored it to show at the World's Fair.

Then, just as mysteriously as at Pomona in 1963, he turned up at the Nostalgia Nationals in Fremont, California that year. I had no idea the car was there until, as I was working on my own car in the pits, I caught a glimpse through the grandstands of this beautiful, unmistakable dragster smoking the tires down the track. Then, as the engine shut off, I heard this collective gasp from the crowd. One of the inexperienced crew had left the string in the chute, the car went off the end of the track, hit a tree, and Jack suffered broken ribs and severe lacerations. He was whisked to a hospital, and the twisted car was loaded up and hauled home. I didn't see or know any of this at the time, except that the car had crashed, and left.

So I made a point of finding out what had become of Jack Williams and *Syndicate Scuderia* for this book. It wasn't easy, but it was rewarding.

Jack is a resilient, as well as talented, guy. After healing his wounds, he set to work rebuilding the car once again. He said he had to remake everything from the engine forward, including the frame, axle, suspension, and body. As you can see in the recent photos, the car not only looks as good as ever, but it runs just as strong. The photo of it with the wheels in the air was taken at Sechelt drag strip in 2001, on Jack's 70th birthday, with Jack at the throttle. That's a mystery story with a happy ending.

Back From the

This chapter is primarily visual, so I won't waste a whole lot of words on it. The "before" and "after" photos are certainly graphic. These are cars that by all rights should have been lost. That they have been saved is a testament to talented and determined individuals. The fact that they are all customs is perhaps telling.

I think that hot rods are easier to keep and to restore. Customs were built to be beautiful, with curvaceous bodies and luscious paint. If those curves got dented or crushed, or the striking paint became cracked and faded, the car's beauty was damaged and its reason for being was at least compromised. Also, custom cars, especially classic customs of the 1940s to 1960s, completely fell out of favor for a few decades. So there was little incentive to keep one up, or to fix it up if it became faded and worn—let alone scratched, dented, crashed, or burned.

Finally, nearly all customs are big cars with yards and yards of sheetmetal, so repairing one that has been damaged or left to rot is a major undertaking. Just repainting one in candies or pearls is a huge job. Those obstacles make what you see in this chapter simply amazing.

Wreckage
Chapter Eight

El Matador

Bill Cushenberry's *El Matador* full custom 1940 Ford coupe was his debut vehicle in 1961. Much has already been written about this car in its original form, as well as its incredible restoration (which was chronicled in five parts in *Custom Rodder* magazine in 1993–1994), plus you can find all sorts of information and photos of it on the Internet (a small portion of which I'd have to question). Suffice it to say that, given this car and a handful of others, Cushenberry should be esteemed at the highest level of great custom craftsmen. The fact that he built so few cars and shied from self-promotion are undoubtedly reasons that he often isn't.

In brief, Cushenberry built this chopped, channeled, sectioned, and resculptured 1940 Ford (with design input from Don Varner) as his new calling card when he moved his custom shop from Wichita, Kansas, to Monterey, California. At the time, its Oldsmobile engine was about the most traditional part of this radical custom. After achieving his goal with numerous magazine covers and big show awards, Bill sold the car to promoter Bob Larivee, who in turn sold it to the AMT model company, which continued showing it in partnership with Ford's Cavalcade of Customs (and for which the Olds engine was swapped for a small-block Ford), although it never made a model of the car.

After changing hands a couple more times (supposedly being sold at one point for $1,700!), it ended up at Florida customizer John McNally's "in the 1970s." He sold the car, bought it back, reportedly restored it once, and then his garage/shop caught fire with the car inside. As you can see from the photos, not only was the car burned, and most of the lead melted out, but the roof was also caved in by the falling garage. Supposedly this happened in the early 1990s, but even considering being burned to bare metal, doused with fire hoses, then left to sit outside in Florida atmosphere, it's hard to imagine the severity of rust apparent in the photos (especially inside the trunk) in that short time.

It's a moot point, because trying to salvage any steel-bodied vehicle that has been warped and annealed (and then quenched with water) in a severe fire is a Herculean task. The team of Harold Murphy and Mike Scott of West Palm Beach, known as Murphy and The Striper to the custom community, acquired the charred-and-twisted hulk you see here in 1993, and painstakingly rebuilt it into the brilliant candy-red restored version seen in the last two photos (courtesy of Luke Karosi of *Customs Illustrated* magazine). Having to literally replace much of the body, interior, and hard-to-find detail parts, they tried to keep it as faithful to the original 1961 version as possible. The only major deviation was the substitution of a 5.0L engine, driveline, and complete suspension from a late-model Mustang to make this custom truly drivable. And that's what they've been doing—fully enjoying this historic, reborn custom—ever since.

Rod & Custom Dream Truck

Next to the Hirohata Merc, *Rod & Custom Dream Truck* is probably the most popular—certainly most well-known—custom of all time. It was actually dreamed up by initial *Rod & Custom* Editor Spence Murray. But the plan was to make it "everybody's custom" by soliciting ideas for custom changes from the readers at large, and then taking the truck to several well-known customizers to let each do his particular modifications to the 1950/1954 Chevy pickup. All of that has been very well documented, first in many issues of *Rod & Custom* (the truck was redone four times), and several places since. This truck even lays claim to the first small-block Chevy V-8 engine swap, done in late 1954.

You probably also know full well that it met its reported "demise" in a cornfield west of Wichita in 1958. While being flat-towed to a show in Des Moines behind a new pickup, both vehicles flipped off the road, the tow truck landing on its roof while the *Dream Truck* "pirouetted on its right front fender, then slammed on its left side, bending the driver's door all the way back," according to one account. After getting an estimate of $3,500 (in 1958 dollars) from Barris to fix it, less paint, owner Spence stripped it of engine, trans, wheels and tires, gauges, etc., and sold the remains for $150, expecting never to see it again.

However, when Spence returned briefly as *Rod & Custom* editor in 1967, he unsuccessfully tried to locate the truck's remains. Possibly because of this, freelancer Michael Lamm sent in some black-and-white photos of the truck, with the body crudely hammered out with a large ball-peen or sledge hammer, where he happened to see it sitting in front of someone's house in Stockton, California. He didn't get an address or talk to the owner. But this sparked Bruce Glasscock, who loves "car tracking." Given a general location of the neighborhood by Lamm, and using clues in the photo backgrounds, he drove up from SoCal and literally did a door-to-door search in Stockton until he found it. But that wasn't enough. The owner wouldn't sell. So Bruce called him every three months for eight years before he finally relented!

Of course once he got it home to Westminster, California, he was faced with fixing it. Spence helped arrange to have metal man Carl Green come out from Oklahoma to work on it and, using pieces from a donor truck, they got it finessed back into shape, reconstructed mechanically, and repainted and upholstered in time for Bruce and Spence to drive it to the first KKOA Nats in Wichita in 1981, as you see it in the "finished" photo. But wait, there's more.

Glasscock likes finding cars more than keeping them, so Barris custom collector Kurt McCormick was able to talk him out of this at-least-partially-Barris-built custom about 10 years ago, and proceeded to have the truck completely restored once again. Unfortunately, I don't have a good photo of this famous custom in its current form, but it is being well-kept, among peers, in the McCormick stable. And this vignette serves as one somewhat-extreme example of how to go about finding lost hot rods.

The Sam Barris Buick

Another famous early custom that was salvaged from the wreckage, and now resides in the Kurt McCormick stable, is the Sam Barris chopped 1950 fastback Buick. It was considered the first of the GM "sedanette" bodies to be chopped, which requires considerable slicing and dicing of the trunk to make it all fit.

This car was featured on the February 1954 cover of *Rod & Custom*, and was sold shortly thereafter by Sam, reportedly to finance eye surgery for his son, John. What this car's life might have been, and how it ever ended up in the woods of Taunton, Massachusetts, in the condition shown, is a complete mystery. However, according to my research, it was discovered there, rusting on the ground with weeds and trees growing through it, either by Bob McCormick or Chris Carrier (another "car finder" who owned the *California Kid* 1934 for a spell). Then it was acquired by 1980s custom-car collector/restorer Jim Walker of Dayton, Ohio, who wisely purchased a low-mile original 1950 Buick sedan (since the chassis and running gear of Sam's car was all stock), and had metal man Dave Oakes graft Sam's surprisingly intact body onto the less-molested chassis and floorpan.

After finding and restoring rare trim parts such as 1953 Pontiac wagon taillights, a 1951 Cad rear bumper, a 1951 Buick front bumper, 1953 Buick headlights, and a 1953 Olds grille, Oakes and Ernie Ball painted the car 1970 Buick Titan Red to match the original metallic lacquer, and the interior was trimmed in buttoned red velour and white Naugahyde rolls to replicate what had been done by the Carson Top Shop in 1953. Kurt, who is not a man of many words, stated, when the car was featured in the February 1993 *Rod & Custom*, "I bought the Buick in 1984 and I've owned it ever since."

1963 Beauty

To bring the prospect of such a project closer to home, here are a couple of photos of a so-called lost custom that turned up at the 2009 KKOA Leadsled Spectacular in Salina, Kansas. As you can see, this chopped, full-custom 1957 Chevy graced the covers of *Car Craft* and *Custom Rodder* magazines in 1963 when it was coated in candy-red paint. Regardless of where and how it was saved over the last 40-some years, just consider what it would take to restore this car, given the crunched left rear quarter and what I can see of lower body rust. Would you want to do it?

Candy Wagon

For the most part, I have shown rods or customs that were lost, but have been found. In Chapter Nine, I show a few that seem to be gone for good. This one falls somewhere in between.

Customized by Joe Bailon and painted in his characteristic candy-apple red with gold-outline scallops, it was first seen in the form shown in the "before" photo on the cover of the February 1958 *Custom Cars* magazine, with a four-page feature inside photographed by George Barris. The car belonged to Bob Pallidino, who named it *Candy Wagon*. The mild customizing was obviously done when the car was brand new. It included double 1956 Buick taillight lenses frenched in the rear fenders, dechroming, frenched-and-peaked headlights with aerials sunk horizontally in the front fenders, and an extended lip over the stock grille. And, though Pallidino's hometown was not mentioned,

the car wore a license frame from the Buick dealer in Antioch, in northern California.

The photos of the car in more dilapidated condition were taken by avid custom builder John D'Agostino at Pallidino's farm somewhere in northern California in 1994 or 1995. In a small item that ran in the April 1995 issue of *Rod & Custom*, it stated that the car was next painted black with lime-gold fogging, and the original grille was replaced with 1953 DeSoto teeth. Finally, it was repainted in candy tangerine before it was retired to this spot "beneath a drippy tree." That was some 15 years ago. I don't know if it's still there or not.

This is one you can trace if you're so inclined. But the main reason I'm showing these photos is to demonstrate that these cars are still sitting, waiting to be salvaged, and because candy tangerine looks so good, even in patina.

Lost and Found

ne of the keynotes of this book is to show you rods and customs that are found, more than lost. That is, I have shown once-lost or forgotten vehicles that exist today and are also accessible in one way or another. As you'll see in Chapter Eleven, some of these cars are lost in plain sight. In other cases, you just need to know where to look to find them—perhaps in your neighbor's garage. But I have made it a point not to include cars that are ensconced in someone's private collection. I could write a whole book on such cars today, but what's the point if you can't go see them?

So this chapter is about once "lost" rods and customs that have turned up, thankfully, in public museums. First I should note that, while automotive museums have been common and plentiful around the world for decades, virtually none, until lately, included hot rods or custom cars. There have been museums of various types of race cars, sure, but only recently have we seen the development of the Garlits and NHRA museums devoted primarily to drag racing. Their collections are pretty well known by now.

What I want to focus on in this chapter are one or two well-known cars in unlikely museums, three or four recent acquisitions by the Petersen Automotive Museum, and several lost gems among the huge, wonderful assortment of rods, customs, and drag race cars assembled by Ralph Whitworth for his proposed new museum in Winnemucca, Nevada. I went to Winnemucca and photographed six of these cars that have little-known, but special historic significance.

Unfortunately, however, hopes and plans for this special museum came crashing down along with the stock market and several financial institutions Ralph worked for or with during the fall of 2009. The worst part is that these cars were sold at auction and are now hidden away again in private collections. So this chapter is brief.

DON'T MISS IT!
AWARD CEREMONIES
Hear Them Roar! - See Them Drive Out!
- SUNDAY NIGHT -
LAST NIGHT OF THE SHOW

XR-6 Roadster

et's start more positively. The 2009 GNRS car show in Pomona had a special building for cars that had been previous Oakland class winners, and three cars showed up there that I hadn't seen in years, but were identified as now belonging to the Petersen Automotive Museum. These were each very significant cars, and I was delighted to see that they would now be preserved and displayed for the public. Mr. Petersen had acquired each of these cars himself, on the museum's behalf, shortly before his death, which makes their inclusion in the collection even more special.

For the *XR-6* roadster to end up at the Petersen is fitting because this was one of the more ambitious, and successful, of all the *Hot Rod* magazine project cars. Spearheaded (and nominally owned) by *Hot Rod* staffer Tex Smith, its mandate was to be "a modern street roadster." In fact, of the many design-concept rods sketched for magazines then (as now), this is the first one actually built.

Starting with a 1927 T turtledeck body and an all-aluminum, Weber-carbed Mopar Slant 6 engine, the car was designed in the then-very-trendy asymmetrical style by Steve Swaja. It was then formed over a square-tube space frame using an original T body and hand-formed steel and aluminum panels by a Barris crew that included Dick Dean and Jack Sutton. It was finished in a red/tangerine Metalflake and trimmed by Tony Nancy.

Its construction was detailed in five issues, culminating with the August 1963 *Hot Rod* cover with Tex chatting with the jet pilot. It was finished just in time for the 1963 Oakland Roadster Show, where it copped the big AMBR trophy. Unfortunately, the leaded fenders and nose were so heavy they kept breaking off. So they were reformed in aluminum by Gene Winfield, the car was repainted in red-tone Metalflake, and it was even retrimmed by Nancy.

Next it was scaled into a 1/25 model kit by AMT, then shipped to the East Coast for a show tour starting in Miami, but was quickly bought by eastern promoter Joe Kizis. After a season of shows, Kizis sold it to one collector in Connecticut, who sold it to another, Malcolm Barlow, who kept it in his small collection about 30 years. When I was able to get photos of it for a feature in the October 1992 issue of *Rod & Custom*, the odometer showed only 317 miles. Barlow died not long after, and the car went through more

hands (but not miles). Petersen was able to acquire it from custom builder/collector/trader Tom Liechty of Ohio.

It probably doesn't have many more miles on it, but the Petersen staff does have it running and actually drove it around for my photo session. Whether you care for the style or not—some do, some don't—you must admit this is a hot rod of historical significance that deserves to be preserved and seen.

The Buttera T Sedan

This brown, boxy 1926 Model T sedan might appear mundane today. But you have to remember a couple of things. First, until he started building it in 1974, Li'l John Buttera was a dragster and Funny Car builder. Second, hot rodding was embedded in its resto-rod era and was still getting used to people actually driving such cars on the highway. So when John turned his attention and considerable fabrication/machining skills to transforming this lowly T into a "1972 Eldorado," the results were breathtaking for the time. But most of what makes this car outstanding is under the skin.

That starts with a hand-fabricated square-tube space frame, on which John hung a custom-machined independent front and rear, coil-over-sprung, disc-braked suspension. To this were mounted chrome knock-off Jaguar wire wheels. Under the splash aprons are Steve Davis-formed, dual aluminum saddle fuel tanks. The 289-ci Ford small-block driveline is nothing special, but unfortunately the air cleaner and A/C

pump cover—custom-milled to match the finned valve covers—are now gone, as is the handmade Babb brass radiator.

The interior carries the Eldo theme with a dash filled with Cadillac gauges, A/C vents, and other conveniences. One mind-blower you can't see here are the plugs in the doorjambs that connect when the doors are closed, and which power the electric windows (when power windows were unheard of in hot rods). John had Tony Nancy finish it in Cadillac fabrics.

Within hours of the car's completion, John jumped in and drove across country to the NSRA Nats and then to Canada. By the time Gray Baskerville photographed it for the December 1974 cover of *Hot Rod*, it already had 30,000 miles on it. It also sat considerably lower, had a chromed grille and headlights, was painted a slightly darker brown, and included a few other things that were captured correctly in Revell's highly detailed 1/25-scale model kit of this car.

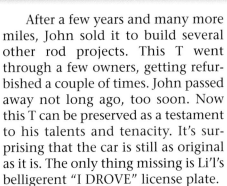

After a few years and many more miles, John sold it to build several other rod projects. This T went through a few owners, getting refurbished a couple of times. John passed away not long ago, too soon. Now this T can be preserved as a testament to his talents and tenacity. It's surprising that the car is still as original as it is. The only thing missing is Li'l's belligerent "I DROVE" license plate.

Barber Car

It was the latter 1960s/early 1970s. Custom cars were dead and gone. Street rods weren't on the street yet. Dragsters and Funny Cars were touring on Pro circuits. If you held a car show, would anybody come? Car people didn't want to see VW buses painted with sunflowers and peace signs (plus hippies didn't care for car shows, anyway). And the real significance of the vans with crystal chandeliers, bars, and tufted boudoir interiors was lost on smaller children, who were a target audience (with their families) of indoor car shows of that era. However, a rolling outhouse with a shingled roof and a crescent moon in the door, or better yet, a bathtub on wheels with a twin-blown Chrysler Hemi, with chrome pipes sticking everywhere, and a real toilet up front for the driver to sit on—now that got the kids' attention.

For the most part these things didn't make the covers of car magazines. It isn't a genre I'm particularly proud of. The bad ones were really bad. But

Many of these creations were dreamed up and built by a company called California Show Cars (CSC), headed by AMBR-winner Bob Reisner and Jay Ohrberg. Not only did they build dozens of these cars, and truck them to shows all over the country in multi-vehicle transporters, they also gave needed employment to many out-of-work name customizers. Dick Dean told me that Ed Newton designed most of them, and *Barber Car* certainly shows the coherent work of a designer's hand.

Dean said he started the car for CSC, but Joe Bailon, who had moved to Hollywood at that time to get

some of the better examples were just a step or two from Roth bubble tops or Dan Woods' *Ice Truck*. *Barber Car* is arguably one of the best of that breed, and I think it's a fitting example to have saved for posterity in the Petersen Automotive Museum. Pete acquired it from Ohio collector Steve Estrin, who absolutely loves these things. The first time I met him, he was telling me with glee how people reacted when he took Roth's *Druid Princess* out for cruises through his neighborhood.

more work, did most of the work on it. You can see, from the custom-built brass radiator and headlights, to the pearl-white wraparound body, to the fully functional, tunnel-ram Chevy engine and Jag independent rear, that this was more than "a bunch of things bolted together" like many of the more frivolous, unrunnable creations were. If you look closely, you'll note a porcelain wash basin with brass faucets behind the antique barber chairs, and those barber poles on the sides light up and rotate. You've gotta love it.

Bailon *Mystery Ford*

Speaking of Joe Bailon, sometime in my long, murky career writing for magazines, someone sent me a snapshot of the Bailon *Mystery Ford,* sitting forlorn and up on wood blocks, in a very small one-car garage. You could only see the front of the car, through the open door, but it was unmistakable. I thought I ran the photo in a "Letters" column, possibly in *Street Rodder* in the 1970s, but I couldn't find it. Of course the sender said the car was going to be restored.

I didn't see it again until I came upon it, totally by surprise, in a diorama on California popular culture at the Oakland Museum of California, situated a stone's throw from the site of the venerable Oakland Roadster Show on Lake Merritt. That part of the diorama included the Bailon '51 Ford, trophies from Oakland, one of the hanging signs from the show, part of a neon Mel's Diner sign, and two excellent early 1970s Arlen Ness choppers. The accompanying photo of that sight was supplied by the museum.

I ran a similar photo in the "Roddin'" column in *Rod & Custom* in October 1992, saying the car, originally built by Bailon for Joe Tocchini in 1957, had finally been restored by Paul McElley. It was nearly as original (including teardrop striping by Tommy the Greek) and was on display for the public to see. The only difference is that Paul painted the roof and lower body silver instead of the original gold, with the candy red in between. I'm not sure why. But if you've ever wondered where this one went, now you know. That display is no longer up, and the car is currently being stored in the museum's vault. But it (and the Ness bikes) should be on display again in the future.

Two final thoughts: First, Joe Bailon built a *lot* of customs, but not many remain, possibly for the simple reason that candy-red lacquer deteriorated quickly. I've reported on sightings of *Candy Bird* a few times. But if you want to know what happened to Joe's original *Miss Elegance* Chevy coupe, see page 60 of the August 1990 *Rod & Custom.*

Second, you never know what you'll find in small museums around the country. Searching on the computer, I discovered that Charlie Ryan's original *Hot Rod Lincoln* Model A was being displayed at a small, county museum in northeast Washington. Since I was going up there to visit Mike Famalette and the *Graffiti* Impala, I had planned to stop and photograph it there. Well, Larry Tarantolo somehow found it first, discovered it was just on loan from the family, and was able to buy it, as shown earlier.

So, whether you're traveling or just 'Net surfing, check out local museums, automotive or otherwise. You just might find a long-lost hot rod or custom.

Gone?

I have shared so many stories of lost hot rods that have been found, one way or another, that I don't want to forget to stress that many searches for such cars end in frustration, if not complete futility. Of course such stories aren't nearly as much fun to tell, so I've minimized them. But don't think that finding lost hot rods is easy. In fact, finding one by mistake, or by surprise, is much easier than trying to find a specific lost car.

There are a few such rods, customs, and race cars that have become almost as famous for being lost as they were otherwise. One prime example is Stuart Hilborn's beautiful, record-setting "streamliner" that ran his first fuel injector. I know it went to a speed shop in Tulsa, then—poof—gone.

Bruce Meyer took out ads in *Rod & Custom* asking for it. Someone else built a clone. And in *The Rodder's Journal* No. 14, Jay Fitzhugh used it to lead off an article titled "Missing," in which he polled several experts to come up with a list of the "10 most wanted" missing rods. He offered a leather *The Rodder's Journal* jacket to anyone who could show proof of finding one. No one did. Besides the Hilborn car, that list included a Westergard 1936 roadster (any), the Du Vall/Kurtis So-Cal Plating 1935 Phaeton "delivery truck," George Barris' first 1941 Buick, the Paul Fitzgerald East Coast 1932 roadster, Bailon's *Miss Elegance*, Mazmanian's 1941 Willys, the Stellings & Hampshire dragster, Barris' *Kopper Kart*, and the Cushenbery *Silhouette*.

I know certain cars are gone, such as *Moonglow* 1954 Chevy and Nick Matranga's 1940 Merc. Others are sequestered, like the *Kookie Kar* and *Golden Sahara*. And the recent discovery of Roth's *Orbitron* in Mexico proves anything's possible. Any of the above might pertain to the following.

Chapter Ten

LeRoy Goulart's 1950 Ford

I've stated on more than one occasion that this lime-gold Ford is my personal favorite shoebox Ford. It's seen here in its first dual-headlight version with Von Dutch striping and in its second iteration with canted quad lights, wheelwell coves, and a one-piece 1952 Ford windshield,. And I've told the story of how LeRoy and fellow customizer Lanny Erickson (builder of the *Violet Fantasy* chopped 1956 Chevy) decided to drive the Ford from Modesto, California, to Erickson's hometown in Minnesota in the dead of winter ("Because we were crazy"). They slid off an icy road in Rawlins, Wyoming, on the way home, punching a hole in the hydro's trans pan, and left the car at a Chrysler dealership there because its shop had an indoor garage.

LeRoy had told me this story a couple times, but I updated it recently in *The Rodder's Journal*, showing a new photo of the car in its final form of white pearl with green fogging around the wheel arches. LeRoy also just told me they weren't totally crazy: "I raised the car up a good half inch before the trip." This was February 1961.

Planning to come back and get the car, LeRoy loaded his tools and boarded a Greyhound bus for home. By the time he got back 24 hours later, his mom had 10 calls from people in Rawlins wanting to buy the car. The only other damage was that the freezing weather had started the lacquer paint to hairline crack in places. So he sold it to the shop manager for $950, who repainted it in cheap green enamel and gave it to his son as a graduation gift. That's all LeRoy knew for years, until Curt Weber, a reader of *The Rodder's Journal*, from Cheyenne, Wyoming, saw the piece and contacted him to say that's where the car ended up. We're not sure how, but Weber says he saw the car in a local show in 1963 or 1964, entered by Ruben Valerio, who had a custom shop there. Next it was sold to Jesse Vasquez, who drove it for a couple years.

Finally, a guy I'll simply say was known as a "borracho" ended up with it and lost it on a tight curve, flipping it into a ravine. Supposedly the smashed roof was cut off, the white T&R interior ended up in a 1955 Ford, and the relatively undamaged custom front end was sold to someone with a 1949–1951 Ford in Las Cruces. No one ever reported seeing a shoebox with that front end in that area, and there was no word on where the tri-carb Olds engine went. But I now can say with some certainty that this famous Ford met its end in a ravine somewhere near Cheyenne around 1965 or 1966. I told you these might not be happy stories.

The Lee & Wells Lincoln

This story simply begins with the wonderful accompanying photo, which I believe I got from Hershel "Junior" Conway. It is, of course, a 1956–1957 Lincoln Continental Mark II, a very rare car that cost nearly $10,000 new. This one was owned by Gary Lee, whom Junior identified as "a radio guy" from Chicago, in some sort of partnership with Lee Wells, a custom upholsterer from North Hollywood, Cali-

fornia. If it had a show name, I don't know what it was. I know it as the "Lee & Wells" custom Continental. It was featured in the July 1965 issue of *Car Craft*, but I don't have that issue to refer to.

Besides the obvious bubble top and full custom interior (with a chrome TV), flared fender lips, and a grille (from a Mercedes) that uncannily predates the 1969-up Mark IIIs and successors, Junior says it was

slightly sectioned (about an inch or two) and that the bodywork was done by "a guy in Burbank." What Junior could tell me for sure was that he painted it Marigold Metalflake. It was one of the first jobs he did in his own shop after leaving Barris', and the first to win a Best Paint award for him at the 1965 Winternationals car show. The car was also awarded Best Interior and first place, Full Custom Coupe & Sedan. After that year on the show circuit, the car simply disappeared.

Junior had heard that it was in the San Diego Automotive Museum, but that was a dead end. I heard from another source that it was in a custom/restoration shop in Indiana, Illinois, or somewhere else in the Midwest, but that's as far as I could get. In fact, I just found a lengthy discussion on the H.A.M.B. Internet site about custom Mark IIs, and, out of nearly 200 responses, only one or two even mentioned this car, and nobody knew its whereabouts. My question is, simply, how could a car like this just disappear? To further the amazement, Lee and Wells preceded this custom with an even more outrageous double-bubble, double-cockpit Top Fuel dragster that appeared on the same cover of *Car Craft* (September 1964) as Ed Roth's *Orbitron*. That one was built by Dick Dean and painted in two shades of candy blue by Junior, but nobody knows where it went, either.

Uncertain T

This crazy car is quite aptly named. In fact, I'm surprised Jay Fitzhugh didn't include it in his list of "10 most wanted." There seems to be a rabid, indefatigable contingent of fans who have been looking for it for the past three or four decades. They are now quite active on the Internet. The most common claim seems to be that it is in an enclosed trailer behind builder Steve Scott's mother's house in Reseda. But everyone who says they know where it is starts by saying they know someone, who knows someone, who—and so on. Well, I actually just talked to someone who went to high school with Steve Scott, and who recently talked to him by phone. But I'm not going to ask him to ask Steve where the T is, or where it went. He's been bugged about it enough. In fact, I won't even tell you where Scott is living, but I can say it's not in North America— nowhere near Reseda.

I think one of the reasons this car continues to create so much interest is because of the model kit that was made of it, and that continues to be sold. Also, like any of Roth's wild creations, it's a unique vehicle that couldn't easily be rebuilt into anything else, and would be pretty hard to make disappear. Even if it were parted out, most any of those parts would be identifiable. So where is it? I have no idea. Others are uncertain too.

Both this car and Steve Scott had a pretty brief but intense career in the hot rod world. Steve built the car by himself, welding up the frame from rectangular tubing and making the body from plywood and fiberglass, as he illustrated with his own photos in a three-page black-and-white feature in the November 1965 issue of *Car Craft*. Adding to this car's mystique, the only color image is a full cover rendering with a blue see-through (or cut-away) body painted or airbrushed over a photograph of a red frame with yellow accents. But the car was never blue. It was first a dark-red candy painted by Bill Cushenbery. But when it was beaten by the Lee & Wells Continental for Best Paint at the 1965 Winternats, Scott had Junior repaint it Nutmeg Metalflake (a brown/red/gold mix), before embarking on a national show tour. Then,

before it disappeared, it got painted the gold Metalflake you see in the third photo here.

Scott was also an avid photographer. He took these pictures, and also freelanced several rod features to magazines for about two years, including the photos of Bob Grossi's T coupe in Chapter Eleven. Not only did he pose pneumatic girls with beehive hairdos in many of his photos, he somehow included himself, as well.

I inherited some of his photography because when he quit, as abruptly as he started, he left it unclaimed. Nobody knew where to contact him, just as nobody seems to really know what happened to his *Uncertain T*. The last I saw of it, it was advertised for sale, with a small black-and-white photo, in the "Rod Mart" section in the back of the July–September 1967 *Hot Rod*, for "$7,000 or eng. $650." An address and phone number is listed in North Hollywood, and the color is stated as "orange 'flake." My assumption is that the car didn't sell, and Scott painted it the gold Metalflake later.

Two things I'd guess: A car like this doesn't just disappear, and, if it were going to show up, we'd surely have seen it by now. However, I'm not really certain—that is, I am *uncertain*—of either conclusion.

The Bettancourt-Zupan Merc

Please forgive the small, grainy pictures. These truly are "spy" photos, but they are of one of the best—and most lost—of the first chopped 1949–1951 Mercs. In fact, this might be *the* first. Louie Bettancourt bought it new in 1949 and took it directly to Gil and Al Ayala to have it chopped, the B-pillars slanted, the "hump" taken out of the fenderline through the door, and the hood corners widely rounded, front and rear. But it never got done, so it went to Barris' for deep burgundy paint and finishing touches like the grille, taillights, and chrome trim. When *Rod & Custom* selected the "Top 20 All-Time Rods and Customs" in August 1990, this was the chopped Merc that made the list as the cleanest, classic representative of the type.

Then, around 1957, Johnny Zupan bought it (see "The George Sein 1932" on page 96 for more on the Zupan Brothers) and took it back to Barris for some "updating" with extra side chrome, bubble skirts with chrome teeth, and copper and bronze two-tone paint. It made the covers of more magazines, but then customs quickly faded away.

The Merc ended up at Dean Jeffries' shop in the Cahuenga Pass next to the Hollywood freeway, where former Barris metalman Bill DeCarr started revising it again with vertical quad headlights and rolled pans, front and rear. After these changes were roughed out, however, Zupan was killed in a work accident, and Jeffries inherited the car. In one photo, you can just see the gray primered, chopped roof between two *Monkee Mobiles* in Jeff's lot.

Unfortunately, customs were dead and the car sat, outside. In fact, by 1970, it was so *passé* that then–*Car Craft* editor Terry Cook did a satirical "road test" on this supposed car club "Moik" in the July 1970 issue. The telling part is that partial photos of the immobile car show the Zupan side chrome on the doors, the reshaped grille/headlight openings, and identifying characteristics such as the uniquely rounded rear hood corners, spotlight mounts in the doors, and the absence of chrome trim around the side windows.

Yet, however *passé* and immobile this Merc, it was plainly visible from the freeway sitting next to Jeffries' shop. Jeff said he was gone to a car show in Long Beach one weekend

night, and returned to find the Merc gone, with two tell-tale skid marks where it was dragged, apparently by a chain, out of his driveway and up Cahuenga Boulevard. But the trail, and the car, was soon completely lost. Rumors began to circulate that a certain notorious motorcycle club was involved, and one of its lawyers in San Francisco was in possession of the car. Obviously, this would be hard to substantiate, and never has been.

However, the "spy" photos shown here were taken, supposedly in front of a gas or towing station in San Francisco, one night many years ago. I got one set from Jeffries, and another (identical) set from custom-phile Barry Mazza in Florida. Nobody seems to know who took them, or exactly when. But you notice the car has blue California plates (from the 1970s) on it, with tags, and accessory taillights, as if for towing. There's even a horn added in the grille (but no headlights). Jeffries says that he got a phone call, years ago, from someone saying he had the car, and wanted to make a deal to get the pink slip for it. But Dean became so angry, he says he just yelled, "I want my @#$% car back," and hung up. He wished he hadn't. But that's the last he's ever heard.

The bottom line? This is the Zupan Merc. Mazza notes you can even see bronze paint on the steering column in the side-window shot, let alone the straight fender line, dechromed windows, rounded hood corner, and spotlight hole in the door. The large peak in the hood is another giveaway. However, beyond these clues, if you look at the 1970 *Car Craft* photos (which I reran in *Rod & Custom* in June 1990), the headlight/grille shell custom work is obviously the same. But all of this, including the spy photos, was decades ago. Dean has never gotten another call. I'll just file this under "California Noir."

Silhouette

As I mentioned in regard to his seminal *El Matador* 1940 Ford, there weren't many Bill Cushenbery customs in the first place, and fewer exist now. *Silhouette*, probably his second most famous car, is simply gone. Built at the height of the bubble-top era in 1962, it made its debut as seen here in pastel-pink pearl fades on a completely hand-formed steel body, at the 1963 Oakland Roadster Show, where it copped the Tournament of Fame award. It was also featured in this form, with Buick wire wheels and an injected nailhead Buick engine, on the cover of the first (and only?) *Petersen Custom Car Yearbook* that year.

Actually I'm a bit confused, because I have another color photo of the car in a rich candy red faded over gold, with white pearl in the coves, with the big AMBR trophy visible behind it with *Twister T* (the 1962 AMBR winner) parked next to it. So Bill possibly repainted the car right before the 1963 Oakland show. At any rate, it won him and his wife a trip to Europe and an invitation to join the Ford Custom Car Caravan, as seen in the other photo. To do so, he had to swap the Buick engine for a Ford, which apparently has two 4-barrels topped with large "baloney slice" chrome stacks. The paint is the darker candy red, with steel dish Astro wheels in place of the chrome wires.

Jay Fitzhugh states that the car was used in a feature film (without stating which one), and it was also

turned into a 1/25-scale plastic model at this time by AMT. Then, by 1968, it was cast as one of the original 16 Mattel Hot Wheels, and remains in that line to this day.

Sometime in the late 1960s or early 1970s, after Cushenbery had moved his shop from Monterey to Burbank, California, the *Silhouette* was reportedly stolen from the back of his lot, and has never been seen again. In fact, someone I know who had a shop in the area at that time, says the rumor was that the car was stolen because of some sort of feud or vendetta, and that it was buried, intact, in a graveyard for stolen and stripped vehicles somewhere in the Valley, and it's probably still there. More "Noir."

Dean Lowe's 1929 Roadster Pickup

To end this chapter on a more positive note: I thought this Roman Red 1929 roadster pickup—one of my favorites—was lost. But I just received photos showing it exists, in pretty original condition, in England, of all places.

Encountering movie stars or other celebrities never excited me much, but seeing a car, for real, that was on the cover of a magazine was a thrill for me as a teen. I saw young Dean Lowe on the cover of the January 1962 *Hot Rod* in a photo very similar to the one shown here (with engine exposed). And then I saw the truck a short time later at the Winternationals, not only running but winning the B/SR class in record time. That was exciting, especially since Dean (at 16) was only a couple years older than I was.

I've always loved full-fendered 1928–1929 A hot rods, especially with dual-quad Corvette engines and 4-speeds, but this one was special for several reasons. First, Dean's father, Buzz, was a hard-core midget racer who had one of the first tube-frame V-8-60 Kurtises. So they took the Model-A frame to Kurtis in Glendale

and had them rework it with an Indy tube front axle, a Halibrand quick change, custom radius rods, a torque arm for the rear, and all tubular cross members. Kurtis' Art Ingels not only built the blistered aluminum hood, he also louvered it, and the splash aprons, and formed the first chromed headers. As far as I know, this is the only hot rod chassis Kurtis built.

Second, "Dyno" Don Nicholson both mentored the build-up of the 'Vette 283 (with Jocko heads, Isky roller cam, Vertex mag, etc.) and helped drive it to the B/SR record at the 1962 W-Nats. The car owned that record for six years, running a best of 11.14 seconds/123 mph at legal weight.

But that wasn't enough for Dean. Seeing John Mazmanian's gorgeous candy-red Willys Gasser at Pomona, he next took the car to Junior's House of Color for a Candy Persimmon paint job, and installed a set of polished Halibrand mags and M&H slicks like Maz'. As seen in the photo from the L.A. Sports Arena car show in May 1962, he also installed a polished 4-71 blower, using a borrowed 2-port Hilborn for the show, but running the dual quads on the blower for street.

Yes, Dean did regularly drive this car on the street, through his senior year of high school and later. But for racing in the quarter- and half-mile drags, as well as at El Mirage, he bolted on Hilborn injectors, along with Belanger headers and a Moon tank, as seen in the later Pomona photo.

By 1965 Dean got married, and their first daughter was born in 1967, so the beautiful and quick pickup was parked in a back corner of the Lowe's L&L Machine shop and it sat right there for 19 years. At least it was well preserved. Then, in 1986, Bruce Geisler, who had his own red 1929 with a blown Chev (notice how the same names keep coming up in this book?), talked Dean into selling him the truck. But all Bruce did was take it apart and store it on pallets in the back of his shop. Hearing this, I called Bruce, but he said he'd sold it to some guy from England 10 years ago, and didn't know who he was.

I found out from Steve Dennish at Limeworks that the guy was Stephen Hill, whom he knew when he lived in England, but it took several tries for me to find him. I almost gave up. But I finally got an email back, with a fuzzy photo of the front of the pickup in a shed.

Stephen had been working for a defense contractor in Kuwait, got offered a job in L.A., which he jumped at, went shopping for a roadster as soon as he got here, and bought the Lowe pickup from Bruce, in pieces, in 1998. He then found out the job wasn't real, so he shipped everything to England. Most of the pickup was on pallets at Bruce's, because he was going to put it on a TCI chassis; but they couldn't find the frame. "Further digging around uncovered the original Kurtis chassis wedged upright on its running board brackets, holding up the fence behind the shop," said Stephen. He also located a 283, T-10 4-speed, and a 1940 rear to ship with the car. However, back home he "relocated from one end of the country to another" for several years, so no progress was made other than bolting the pieces back together as a roller.

Now, says Stephen, he is finally settled in Brighton, and plans to "Start off with getting the car back to how it looked on the January 1962 *Hot Rod* magazine cover." In the recent photo he sent, you can see that much of the Candy Persimmon is still on it, the Schifano top and red upholstery is in surprisingly good condition, and it has the Kurtis chassis and front axle under it. It even has the Belanger headers and the decals in the windshield. He didn't give me a time-frame, but it looks very restorable, and the best part is that this one is finally found, not lost.

Garage Cars

Well, I am nearly out of room. I've almost crossed the finish line, the chute is out, the brakes are beginning to fade, and if I don't get this thing stopped right now, we're going to be off the track and into the weeds. I had intended to include three more chapters, but I have to squeeze them into this one. I told you at the beginning that the main reason for doing this hot rod archaeology was the pure intrigue and enjoyment of it. I still feel that way, and I hope you agree. It has been fun. The only frustration is having to leave so much material on the cutting room floor. Once you start looking for this stuff, there's just so much to find. And for every car, there's an equally fascinating story, only fractions of which I was able to tell in many cases.

Here are a couple of requests: First, if you have a lost hot rod that you think should be in a book like this, hopefully with an intriguing story, let me know. And, second, don't loan this book to your friends. Make them buy their own.

Okay. The title of this chapter is "Garage Cars," which means cars that are lost in people's garages because either they seldom get taken out and driven, or they just never get finished. The car club I currently belong to has a rule that each member must have a running, driving hot rod. But there was a club in the Minnesota Street Rod Association actually named "Garage Cars," whose members all had more-or-less terminal project cars that got worked on in heated garages in the middle of winter, but never seemed to get completed. I have room to speak here because I've just finished a 1932 Ford roadster after 13 years, and my vintage dragster is still in bare metal after being in my garage longer than that. It will get done as soon as this book does.

However, my dragster exemplifies the other chapter I've rolled into this one: "Lost in Plain Sight." Such lost rods could take many forms. But my dragster was perhaps better known as *The Pickle*, Tom Taros' green No. 13 rail that he ran with a nitro-fed Chevy V-8 for decades. I was one of the few who knew it was previously the historic orange-and-black Ike Iacono car, with GMC inline-six power, that was on the *Hot Rod* cover in 1959. Bob Pierson's 1936 Ford coupe is similar today. But other cars are lost in plain sight because of a combination of their being kept in closed garages too much, and their interesting or significant stories therefore remaining unknown to the rodding public. I am here to enlighten you on a couple of these, as well as the perennial garage-kept car, the T-bucket. But I'm running out of track, so let's go.

Chapter Eleven

Doana's Deuce

I started with this one because it's lost in plain sight mainly because it doesn't get out of the garage enough. Plus it's a frustrating example of a car with multiple stories and history that I can only skim here. If you don't know who Doane Spencer was, or his black, V-windshield 1932 hiboy roadster, pick up any hot rod history or "Best Of" book, and you'll find out.

What it might not tell you is this: After the Deuce, Doane, accompanied by his young daughter, Doana, flew to Detroit in early 1955 and drove Thunderbird Number 603 off the assembly line to SoCal. Within days Doane had it disassembled, totally tweaked the dual-quad hi-perf 292 Y-Block, added a 4-speed and Halibrand Indy mags, and drove it to Bonneville where it set records for several years, hitting 149.63 mph by 1961. In 1984 he pulled the Y-Block for an all-new 302, in a 10-year total rebuild (see *Rod & Custom* October 1994). So he gave the 292 and 4-speed, as-is,

to his high school classmate, longtime rodding friend, and fellow Ford-natic (and near-identical T-Bird owner), Fred Stebbins, to put in a 1932 coupe he was building.

Now if you're a *Rod & Custom* reader (or rodder) from the 1970s, you know Fred Stebbins for his hot little handmade fiberglass-bodied, S.Co.T.-blown Crosley-powered roadster that graced the July 1970 *Rod & Custom* cover and won many a "Streetkhana" at rod runs. If not, you surely remember his twin-engine, blown Crosley dragster from early Antique Nationals. Like Doane, he built amazing stuff. For instance, he built the bright-red Deuce seen here from a rare fiber-glass body, which he proceeded to section a deceptive 2½ inches through the middle. He put it on a Ford frame, adding the Spencer 292 and 4-speed, as well as 1970s street rod amenities like heat and A/C. Then, in typical Stebbins/Spencer style, he decided the 4-speed

should be column-shifted, so he somehow did it. It's the only one I've ever seen.

Fred was also a good friend of mine, so I'm sad to say he passed away unexpectedly in October 1996. But he had already made provisions that the 1932 coupe with her dad's engine should go to Doana, and it did. She and her husband, Ernie Raquepo, run a tire service in Atascadero, California, where, as you can see, she keeps in it fine condition. I can also attest, having ridden in it with her, that it runs about as strong as any Y-block I've ever experienced. The only problem is that the car just doesn't get enough exercise. On the other hand, that might be a good thing, because one trait Doana inherited from her father, admittedly, is that she can only drive a performance car one way—scary fast. I can vouch for that in both cases.

The Pierson 1936 Coupe

I was driving through downtown Glendale 10 to 15 years ago when I happened to see this bright-red, low, chopped 1936 Ford street rod blast by. I don't often do this, but it looked so nice I decided to follow it home. It was the only time, before or since, that I saw it driving on the street. Home turned out to be the Mountain Avenue foothills, and the owner was Bill King, a member of the Road Kings of Burbank car club. He eagerly showed me the car's details, including a bright-red interior with billet accessories, a typical small-block Chevy engine, Rootlieb hood sides, and a TCI chassis with a Mustang II suspension. With stock bumpers and lights, billet wheels, and pinstripe graphics along the sides, it was a nice car, but neither unusual nor extraordinary enough to interest any magazine editors in doing a feature on it after I sent them some of the snapshots shown here, which I took in Bill's backyard that day.

It wasn't until after I'd taken the pictures and was about to leave that he casually mentioned that this was the former Bob Pierson car. What? Besides the nicely chopped top, about the only clues were the not-filled roof and rubber running boards. But this was the "Hot Rod of the Month" that graced the cover of the August 1948 issue of *Hot Rod* magazine, running 117 mph at El Mirage before the top was

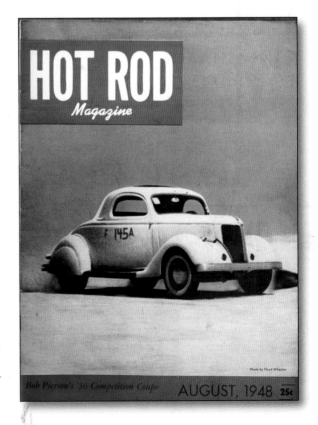

HOT ROD
Magazine

F 145A

Bob Pierson's '36 Competition Coupe   AUGUST, 1948 25¢

Photo by Floyd Wheeler

chopped. The photos were by Pete and the cutaway drawing was by Medley—classic. I can't remember if Bill even told me when or how he got the car, but he did say "the original chassis was junk," and he made it a "good driver."

King passed away in 2007 and the car now belongs to fellow Road Kings member Frank Nay of Burbank. With all the coverage given the restored red/white/blue Pierson Bros. '34 Bonneville coupe, not much has been printed about the 1936 since 1948. I called the number I had for Bob Pierson to ask a few questions, and was told by his wife, Sandra, that Bob left us last April. I did, however, reach his younger brother Dick, who gladly told me that he and Bob chopped the top of the '36 with the help of Harry Jones (who painted 2D), that the sumptuous tan-and-brown Runyan roll-and-pleat interior was retained, along with the chrome dash and column shift, and that the Tokay Beige paint (an off-white) was spotted in. With the chopped top and the race engine in the 1936, it ultimately hit 140 mph at the lakes.

By 1950, as seen at Bonneville in the grainy photo, it was relegated to street duty and towing the race car (it flat-towed it all the way to B-Ville and back; how's that for a combo?). Dick said the car was sold to Don Roush of Big Bear in 1951 or 1952, and all he knows is that it was crashed off an icy mountain road sometime after that (and obviously repaired).

As far as I can remember, Bill King got it in still pretty much original condition. I know he told me he swapped out the 1936 chassis for the TCI replacement. Somehow the original hot-rod-louvered hood sides ended up on Jon Fisher's Calori-style 1936 (see *The Rodder's Journal* No. 10). It's a striking street rod the way it is. Maybe just knowing that it was Bob Pierson's 1948 *Hot Rod* cover car is enough. Would it be better restored to its early configuration? Frank Nay says his plans are to install a Glide seat and air conditioning to make it even more comfortable for street driving.

Grossi's T

The jaunty guy in the red shirt leaning against the chocolate-colored T coupe is Bob Grossi, 45 years ago when this photo was taken by Steve Scott for a feature in *Hot Rod* magazine. That also included Chuck Miller's Hilborn-injected Buick-powered 1927 T roadster ("A Rare Pair," March 1965). Neither Bob nor his T appears much different today, and his hot rod enthusiasm hasn't waned one iota. This is one of the cars that ended up in this book because somebody said, "Oh, if you're looking for cars like that, I know where there's one..." I can't even remember who told me about it, and the only reason it's in this chapter is because it is lost in the ever-changing gaggle of other rods at Grossi's rambling Van Nuys house.

When I arrived, there was a 1954 Ford custom and something else in the driveway, a '40 pickup on the other side of the yard, and in the garage was Bob's current rod-runner—a '34 Ford full-fendered roadster with a dual-quad, GMC-blown big-block. Next to it was a 1969 Camaro SS being worked on, and in front of that was a fully tricked-out 1956 F-100 with another big blown motor, in black. Next to it were three or four more big- and small-block Chevy engines, all with various-size superchargers, on engine stands. Wow. But where was the T coupe?

"Oh, that's out in the back garage," said Bob. So we want through the lushly landscaped backyard decorated with things like old pedal cars and gas pumps, to another wide garage that holds four or five more cars. That TV ad about "Too much good stuff" was beginning to run through my head. Bob unlocked one of the doors, and there it was, looking pretty much like it did when he built it 50 years ago.

Actually, Bob said if I'd arrived four years earlier, it would have looked exactly like it did in that 1965 *Hot Rod* feature. And, he added, the big difference back then was that he built this car on a tight beginning-mechanic's budget in a one-car garage, doing virtually all the work himself. Then, it had a 265 and 3-speed (converted to top-shift by Bob), but he was able to spring for a Cyclone quick-change and enough chrome to cover just about everything under the car. Painted Cherrywood Mahogany with many yards of 1-inch black rolls and pleats—the same upholstery that's in the car now—stitched up right in Bob's garage by Frank Drexler, this was a driver and a show winner.

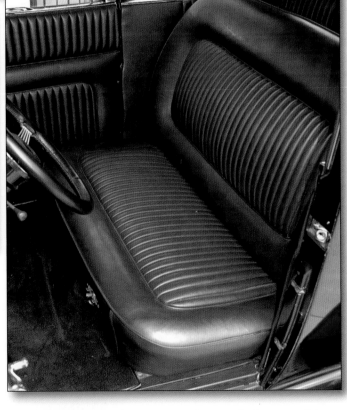

Obviously Bob's attention drifted to several other rod projects (and tons of work he's done on his house and yard), so the tall T sat neglected in the back garage for a few decades. Then, in 2004, he decided it was time to spiff it up a bit. Besides a more contemporary, and very healthy, 383 Chevy, his major upgrade was a big Halibrand Champ Q.C. for the rear, on coil-overs, with Wilwood disc brakes, all narrowed to fit some wide rollers under the back on Eric Vaughn Real Wheels. The rest of the chassis, a boxed T frame with a 1939 Ford tube axle updated with Mustang II disc brakes and Vega steering, remains much the way Bob built it in 1959. The only other change was a fresh coat of Cordovan Brown lacquer sprayed by friend Chuck Minutella.

So Bob's tasty brown T isn't exactly lost, and it doesn't spend all its time in the garage, but it does get pushed into the background by all his other rods and projects. But one thing's for sure: Given that he's had it for 50 years, maintained in show-and-go condition, this one is definitely a keeper.

Leonard Woods' *Vicky*

Where do I start with this one? If you know anything about drag racing, you know about the Stone, Woods, Cook Willys (see Doug Cook's '37 Chevy in Chapter Seven). If you've been to the NHRA Museum, or read hot rod magazines in the last 25 years, you've probably seen the restored, candy-blue, blown-Hemi-powered S-W-C Willys. It is arguably the most famous drag car of all time. It was primarily owned and campaigned by Tim Woods, head of Woods Construction Company in Los Angeles. Fred Stone was a partner and PR genius who started the "Gasser Wars," promoting this car into the first Pro Touring drag machine that won major events and ran match races all across the USA in the early to mid 1960s. Doug Cook was the driver/tuner.

But the middle name on the side of the car read "Leonard Woods, Jr." Who was he? He was Timothy L. Woods' son, a scrawny (but bright) kid who was just beginning studies at Notre Dame University in Indiana about the time the S-W-C coupe was starting to tour the country. His dad made him a part of the team, at least nominally, and "Lenny" did join the crew whenever the car was racing in the Midwest and

on his summer breaks. However, the Gasser Wars in general, and the S-W-C Willys team in particular, came to a screeching halt (supplanted by Fuel Funny Cars), just about the time Leonard graduated from college, so he secured a position with Ford Motor Company to begin his personal career.

Much later, in the 1980s, I heard through channels that Leonard Woods, Jr., owned a Ford dealership in Chino, California, which he had recently moved to the more-upscale suburban Chino Hills. But he didn't put his name on it. It's just Chino Hills Ford. He's not the typical car salesman who goes on TV to hawk his products. He's more of a background type of guy.

So I wasn't sure what to think when someone I didn't know came up to me at some event and showed me snapshots of this beautiful, candy-blue, slightly chopped 1932 Ford Victoria and told me he had just finished building it for Leonard Woods, Jr. Really? Well that was 4 or 5 years ago, and I had never seen the car anywhere, so I wasn't sure if it was even true. This one falls in the category of "Lost in plain sight."

Remembering this, I called Chino Hills Ford and asked for Leonard. It took a few tries, but I finally got

Car builder/racer Mike Van Sant, who has been working for Leonard Woods at the Ford dealership since 1982.

I can't tell you the exact order of events, but Denny found a formerly rodded 1932 Victoria and Mike somehow hooked him up to completely rebuild it for Leonard. It was Lenny's idea to mildly chop the top, paint it "S-W-C Blue," and put a big, blown, Gasser-style motor under the hood—but a Ford, of course. Van Sant was in charge of building the 351W-based mill with SVO heads, a steel crank, Arias pistons, and an Engle cam (what else?). It also has an Accel crank-trigger ignition that allowed Don Hampton to build a low-profile manifold to keep the 6-71 and dual 600-cfm Holleys under the three-piece 1932 hood. The chassis uses a built C-4, hefty chrome Currie 9-inch rear, and a Super Bell tube front axle and disc brakes. The contemporary interior is stitched in bone leather over T-Bird Turbo Coupe seats. The car is stunning, as you can see, and runs and drives as good as it looks—thanks to Van Sant's tuning.

This left just one question for me: Did Leonard have previous hot rods? "Oh, yes. A 1957 T-Bird with a big 394-ci Olds mill and a B&M hydro." It was his street driver/racer back in the day, with "several paint jobs by Ruben, just like the race car." And, yes, he still has it. Another lost hot rod. Another story.

him on the phone, told him who I was, and asked if he had a 1932 Victoria. "Sure do," was the reply. It took a little more doing to get together to take pictures at his place in Chino, but as you see, I did. This car should be on the covers of magazines, or winning show trophies. But Leonard keeps it in his garage and takes it out to drive once in a while.

The guy who showed me the snapshots must have been Denny Russell of Dayton, Indiana, who has a shop called Denny's Rods & Customs. He's a former Fuel Altered racer and friend of longtime Funny

Mike's T-Bucket

I was going to include a whole chapter on T-bucket roadsters in this book, because they tend to be the quintessential garage cars. I really don't know why; but they are.

Of course Model T roadster hot rods come in every shape, style, and configuration possible, and I've already shown a couple that fit in prior categories. But you know what I mean when I say "T-bucket": It's typically a fiberglass body with an abbreviated, integral pickup bed, mounted on a simple ladder-style rectangular tube frame, with a beam or tube axle mounted suicide-style up front, and followed by some sort of big, often blown engine. No hood, no fenders, big-n-little tires and wheels. Most of them derive directly from Norm Grabowski's and Tommy Ivo's famous prototypes. And, depending entirely on how the builder hangs these simple components together, and how many extra trinkets are added to the package, these cars can look simple and sleek, mean and nasty, or cockeyed and silly.

Mike Kennedy's cobalt-blue example from San Clemente, California, fits the first two of those descriptions, leaning more toward the simple and sleek. The mean and nasty part is the big Chrysler Hemi engine, which was actually the starting point of this car. I'm presenting it because it's an excellent example of proportion, stance, and simplicity in a

home-built T-bucket, without losing any of the distilled hot rod flavor that is the primal essence of this type of car. On the other hand, it's in this chapter, representing T-buckets in general, because it had exactly 4 miles on its odometer before I arrived to take pictures.

Mike got inspired to build this car when he read an article, in the December 1988 issue of *Rod & Custom*, on how to build a pared-down version of an early Chrysler Hemi for a street rod. Within months he scored a 1955 300-series 331, complete with the factory dual-quad intake setup, for $150 at the Pomona swap meet, and started the project. That was 20 years ago.

Mike had known Jerry Keifer of T-bucket specialists California Custom Roadsters (CCR) longer than that, so the two collaborated to build a custom frame of Mike's design on the CCR jig, to mount the Hemi engine. They adapted a Turbo-350 trans and 1955 Chevy rear end. The body is a standard CCR fiberglass unit, and even the interior comes from CCR as a ready-to-install kit.

Mike works as a mechanic every day, and helps crew on the Bob McKray/Don Enriquez Junior Fuel dragster on the weekends, so he had no problem

building the engine and assembling the car in his garage at home. In fact, by 1993 he had the car basically assembled and running, less paint and upholstery. But then, well, there are many reasons for the garage-car syndrome. A certain type of rodder likes the building of the project more than the finishing, or using, of it. In Mike's case, working on cars all day and most weekends doesn't leave a lot of time, or inclination, to do more in his free time at home. He'd rather be surfing (as the license frame says).

For whatever reason, it took Mike until now to get the car done. As you can see from the photo, the odometer now has about 40 more miles on it (though Mike admits they're not all "linear"). But since this photo session he still hasn't gotten it insured and licensed. That's the part of the T-bucket thing I don't understand. Sure, they're not as comfortable as a coupe or even a 1932–1934 roadster; but they're better than a motorcycle, and at least as exciting. That's what T-buckets are all about: wind, noise, spinning tires, everything hanging out in the breeze—pure, essential hot rod. Mike, you live just a couple blocks from Pacific Coast Highway—get your roadster out there and run it!

Larry Wood's Zoomy Coupe

Our final entry is more like the classic case of the cobbler's kids' shoes. As you undoubtedly know, Larry Wood has had an illustrious career as chief designer for Mattel Hot Wheels, those wild and zany, far-out little toy cars. He's an Art Center design-school graduate, a pioneering member of the Early Times car club, and the owner/builder of a wide variety of hot rods of his own. You can see his magnificent 1932 Nash Brougham in the background, which graced the cover of the August 1973 *Rod & Custom*, and which he recently completely rebuilt with big-block Chevy power (another lost/found rod). Besides that, Larry has done everything from penning T-shirt and poster designs, to magazine "sketch pads," to wonderful flame layouts on many friends' rods, to designing some of the wildest show machines of the 1970s and 1980s for promoters like Bob Larivee.

As I write this, he was sketching ideas for Carroll Shelby's latest interpretation of a Ford Mustang, as well as building the interior for a 1940s-era, fifth-wheel aluminum house trailer to tow behind his just-completed, fully hot rodded 1940s Ford COE tractor.

He's had his own well-equipped (and well-decorated) hobby shop in Long Beach for many years, just a couple blocks from Mickey Thompson's former speed emporium, and he's always had multiple fun projects in various stages of construction.

The only thing Larry hadn't done was to design and build one of these far-out hot rods for himself, and by himself. So that's what he decided to do, more than 25 years ago. Larry said he's always loved 1934 three-window coupes, so he started with one of Ai Fiberglass' then-new chopped 1934 bodies, and started sketching ideas for "Something high-tech that still looked like a hot rod." He also wanted to "Build every piece on the car, like Dan Woods or Boyd." And finally, "I wanted to make it *my* car." You have to remember this was just after Pete Chapouris', Jim Jacobs', and Jim Ewing's coupes hit the rod scene, and chopped 1934 three-windows were the hottest thing going.

The design Larry came up with was like taking Ewing's *Super Bell* coupe to the next planet—a typical Larry Wood far-out hot rod. The fact that he put the blown V-6 engine in the back (sideways) and put the radiators in the Testarossa-like rear-wheel wing-pods, allowed him to make the pointed nose any size and shape he wanted. It blends the best elements of a fenderless chopped hot rod, an aero Bonneville coupe, and a rocket ship.

Larry's shop is equipped with a Heliarc welder and a Bridgeport mill, and he knows how to use them. He started with a pair of 1934 Ford side rails, a bunch of chrome-moly round tubing, and a one-off Buick Grand National V-6 with a Fiero bellhousing, mated to a Fiero 4-speed transaxle. He built a chassis on the floor, incorporating torsion bars and disc brakes front and rear, with handmade IRS in back, but with a hot-rod dropped-tube axle in front. BDS made a manifold to mount a 4-71 blower, with two Weber carbs, and Larry crafted the GP-style 6-into-1 header himself. He stole the whale tail on the deck from a Porsche, but for the nose he carved a plug out of foam, made a mold, and cast his own part.

Most guys who draw far-out cars (or write about them) don't have a clue how to actually build them. But after designing this thing, Larry set to work cutting, welding, and fabricating the chassis; designing and building the suspension, steering, and brakes; mounting the engine and transaxle; plumbing the car; and even molding his own body parts. All this took place fairly quickly. However, Larry recently admitted that building this car was kind of like the way he used to build plastic model kits. He'd put the body, chassis, wheels/tires, and engine together; move them around, reshape them; get it to look and sit the way he wanted; but then he'd lose interest when it came time to add all the little details to finish it.

That's pretty much where this car stopped a couple decades ago. It got pushed into a corner as new and different projects took its place. Now it's back in the middle of the floor, and Larry is installing flush-mount plexi side windows like a Bonneville car and is thinking about a silver paint scheme with hand-painted rivets, aircraft-style. "But," he admits, "This might be as far as it gets." He'd really rather finish up that aircraft-style travel trailer and take it out on the road behind its tangerine-and-silver-pearl COE. We'll see.

Afterword

Okay, I have to stop. There are plenty more of these cars and stories. If you have one I should know about, let me know. Otherwise, if you have a hot rod to build, build it. If you have one that's finished and ready to drive, drive it. Or, if there are other lost hot rods to be found, go and find them.

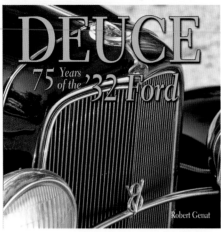
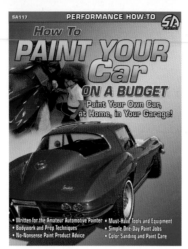
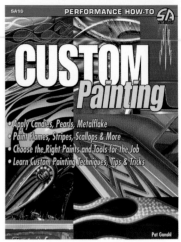
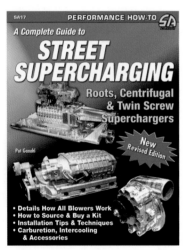
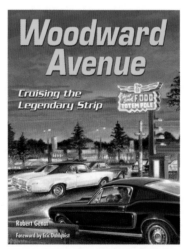
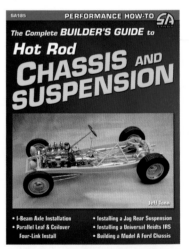